GOLF RULES ILLUSTRATED

ELEVENTH EDITION

COMPILED BY
R&A RULES LIMITED

ILLUSTRATIONS BY
**PETER DAVIDSON, HELIX DESIGN PARTNERSHIP
AND LINE+LINE**

hamlyn

Foreword

This new edition of the ever-popular Golf Rules Illustrated incorporates the new Rules of Golf effective from January 2004. These new Rules reflect a linguistic review of the entire Rule Book, an expanded Etiquette section and numerous modifications designed to achieve consistency of approach and where possible simplification of the Rules.

Golfers will understand that, in a game which depends on a high degree of sportsmanship and self regulation, a reasonable working knowledge of the Rules of the game is not only necessary but can often be advantageous.

Golf Rules Illustrated is a user-friendly guide to the Rules and highlights, by a series of illustrations and incidents taken from actual tournament play, commonly encountered situations which all golfers, irrespective of their playing ability, should find helpful in expanding their understanding of the Rules of this great game. I hope you will enjoy reading and referring to it.

W. MICHAEL B. BROWN
Chairman, Rules of Golf Committee,
R&A Rules Limited

R&A Rules Limited

The Royal and Ancient Golf Club of St Andrews is transferring to R&A Rules Limited, with effect from 1st January 2004, the responsibilities and authority of The Royal and Ancient Golf Club of St Andrews in making, interpreting and giving decisions on the Rules of Golf.

The new Rules of Golf have, therefore, been approved by R&A Rules Limited. As from 1st January 2004, the Rules of Golf shall be made, altered, interpreted and applied by R&A Rules Limited.

Gender

In the Rules of Golf, the gender used in relation to any person is understood to include both genders.

Golfers with Disabilities

The R&A publication entitled "A modification of the Rules of Golf for Golfers with Disabilities", that contains permissible modifications of the Rules of Golf to accommodate disabled golfers, is available through the R&A.

CONTENTS

SECTION 1
ETIQUETTE; BEHAVIOUR ON THE COURSE

INTRODUCTION
This section provides guidelines on the manner in which the game of golf should be played. If they are followed, all players will gain maximum enjoyment from the game. The overriding principle is that consideration should be shown to others on the course at all times.

THE SPIRIT OF THE GAME
Unlike many sports, golf is played, for the most part, without the supervision of a referee or umpire. The game relies on the integrity of the individual to show consideration for other players and to abide by the Rules. All players should conduct themselves in a disciplined manner, demonstrating courtesy and sportsmanship at all times, irrespective of how competitive they may be. This is the spirit of the game of golf.

SAFETY
Players should ensure that no one is standing close by or in a position to be hit by the club, the ball or any stones, pebbles, twigs or the like when they make a stroke or practice swing.

Players should not play until the players in front are out of range.

Players should always alert greenstaff nearby or ahead when they are about to make a stroke that might endanger them.

If a player plays a ball in a direction where there is a danger of hitting someone, he should immediately shout a warning. The traditional word of warning in such situations is "fore".

CONSIDERATION FOR OTHER PLAYERS
No Disturbance or Distraction Players should always show consideration for other players on the course and should not disturb their play by moving, talking or making unnecessary noise.

Players should ensure that any electronic device taken onto the course does not distract other players.

On the teeing ground, a player should not tee his ball until it is his turn to play.

Players should not stand close to or directly behind the ball, or directly behind the hole, when a player is about to play.

On the putting green On the putting green, players should not stand on another player's line of putt or, when he is making a stroke, cast a shadow over his line of putt.

Players should remain on or close to the putting green until all other players in the group have holed out.

Scoring In stroke play, a player who is acting as a marker should, if necessary, on the way to the next tee, check the score with the player concerned and record it.

PACE OF PLAY
Play at Good Pace and Keep Up Players should play at a good pace. The Committee may establish pace of play guidelines that all players should follow.

It is a group's responsibility to keep up with the group in front. If it loses a clear hole and it is

When taking a practice swing, a player should always make sure that no one is standing where they might be hit.

If a group is holding up the players behind and has lost more than a hole on the players in front, it should invite them to play through.

delaying the group behind, it should invite the group behind to play through, irrespective of the number of players in that group.

Be Ready to Play Players should be ready to play as soon as it is their turn to play. When playing on or near the putting green, they should leave their bags or carts in such a position as will enable quick movement off the green and towards the next tee. When the play of a hole has been completed, players should immediately leave the putting green.

Lost Ball If a player believes his ball may be lost outside a water hazard or is out of bounds, to save time, he should play a provisional ball.

Players searching for a ball should signal the players in the group behind them to play through as soon as it becomes apparent that the ball will not easily be found. They should not search for five minutes before doing so. Having allowed the group behind to play through, they should not continue play until that group has passed and is out of range.

PRIORITY ON THE COURSE

Unless otherwise determined by the Committee, priority on the course is determined by a group's pace of play. Any group playing a whole round is entitled to pass a group playing a shorter round.

CARE OF THE COURSE

Bunkers Before leaving a bunker, players should carefully fill up and smooth over all holes and foot-prints made by them and any nearby made by others. If a rake is within reasonable proximity of the bunker, the rake should be used for this purpose.

Repair of Divots, Ball-Marks and Damage by Shoes Players should carefully repair any divot holes made by them and any damage to the putting green made by the impact of a ball (whether or not made by the player himself). On completion of the hole by all players in the group, damage to the putting green caused by golf shoes should be repaired.

Preventing Unnecessary Damage Players should avoid causing damage to the course by removing divots when taking practice swings or by hitting the head of a club into the ground, whether in anger or for any other reason.

Players should ensure that no damage is done to the putting green when putting down bags or

Always repair divots (top right), carefully repair pitch marks on the putting green (bottom left) and smooth over footprints and other marks when leaving a bunker (bottom centre). Do not lean on your putter when removing the ball from the hole (middle right).

the flagstick. In order to avoid damaging the hole, players and caddies should not stand too close to the hole and should take care during the handling of the flagstick and the removal of a ball from the hole. The head of a club should not be used to remove a ball from the hole.

Players should not lean on their clubs when on the putting green, particularly when removing the ball from the hole.

The flagstick should be properly replaced in the hole before the players leave the putting green.

Local notices regulating the movement of golf carts should be strictly observed.

CONCLUSION; PENALTIES FOR BREACH

If players follow the guidelines in this section, it will make the game more enjoyable for everyone.

If a player consistently disregards these guidelines during a round or over a period of time to the detriment of others, it is recommended that the Committee considers taking appropriate disciplinary action against the offending player. Such action may, for example, include prohibiting play for a limited time on the course or in a certain number of competitions. This is considered to be justifiable in terms of protecting the interest of the majority of golfers who wish to play in accordance with these guidelines.

In the case of a serious breach of etiquette, the Committee may disqualify a player under Rule 33-7.

SECTION 2
DEFINITIONS

The Definitions are listed alphabetically and, in the *Rules* themselves,
defined terms are in *italics*.

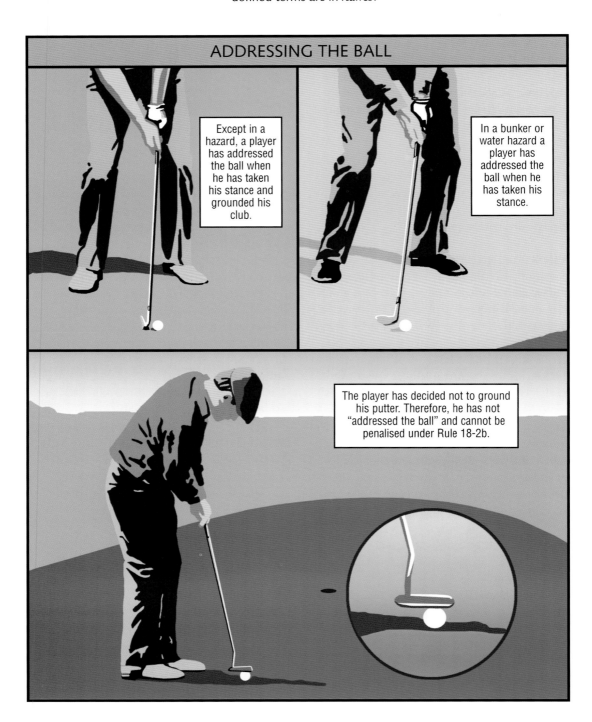

ADDRESSING THE BALL

Except in a hazard, a player has addressed the ball when he has taken his stance and grounded his club.

In a bunker or water hazard a player has addressed the ball when he has taken his stance.

The player has decided not to ground his putter. Therefore, he has not "addressed the ball" and cannot be penalised under Rule 18-2b.

Abnormal Ground Conditions An *"abnormal ground condition"* is any *casual water, ground under repair* or hole, cast or runway on the *course* made by a *burrowing animal*, a reptile or a bird.

Addressing the Ball A player has *"addressed the ball"* when he has taken his *stance* and has also grounded his club, except that in a *hazard* a player has *addressed the ball* when he has taken his *stance*.

Advice *"Advice"* is any counsel or suggestion that could influence a player in determining his play, the choice of a club or the method of making a *stroke*.

Information on the *Rules* or on matters of public information, such as the position of *hazards* or the *flagstick* on the *putting green*, is not *advice*.

Ball Deemed to Move See *"Move or Moved"*.

Ball Holed See *"Holed"*.

Ball Lost See *"Lost Ball"*.

Ball in Play A ball is *"in play"* as soon as the player has made a *stroke* on the *teeing ground*. It remains *in play* until it is *holed*, except when it is *lost, out of bounds* or lifted, or another ball has been *substituted* whether or not the substitution is permitted; a ball so *substituted* becomes the *ball in play*.

If a ball is played from outside the *teeing ground* when the player is starting play of a hole, or when attempting to correct this mistake, the ball is not *in play* and Rule 11-4 or 11-5 applies. Otherwise, *ball in play* includes a ball played from outside the *teeing ground* when the player elects or is required to play his next *stroke* from the *teeing ground*.

Exception in match play: *Ball in play* includes a ball played by the player from outside the *teeing ground* when starting play of a hole if the opponent does not require the *stroke* to be cancelled in accordance with Rule 11-4a.

Best-Ball See *"Matches"*.

Bunker A *"bunker"* is a *hazard* consisting of a prepared area of ground, often a hollow, from which turf or soil has been removed and replaced with sand or the like.

Grass-covered ground bordering or within a *bunker* including a stacked turf face (whether grass-covered or earthen), is not part of the *bunker*. A wall or lip of the *bunker* not covered with grass is part of the *bunker*.

The margin of a *bunker* extends vertically downwards, but not upwards. A ball is in a *bunker* when it lies in or any part of it touches the *bunker*.

Burrowing Animal A *"burrowing animal"* is an animal that makes a hole for habitation or shelter, such as a rabbit, mole, groundhog, gopher or salamander.

BUNKER

A bunker face consisting of stacked turf (whether grass covered or earthen) is not part of the bunker.

CADDIE

A caddie will carry a player's clubs and offer advice on club selection, the direction of play and line for putting.

CASUAL WATER

Casual water is an 'abnormal ground condition' and a player may take relief from such a condition under Rule 25-1.

Note: A hole made by a non-burrowing animal, such as a dog, is not an *abnormal ground condition* unless marked or declared as *ground under repair*.

Caddie A *"caddie"* is one who assists the player in accordance with the *Rules*, which may include carrying or handling the player's clubs during play.

When one *caddie* is employed by more than one player, he is always deemed to be the *caddie* of the player whose ball is involved, and *equipment* carried by him is deemed to be that player's *equipment*, except when the *caddie* acts upon specific directions of another player, in which case he is considered to be that other player's *caddie*.

Casual Water *"Casual water"* is any temporary accumulation of water on the *course* that is visible before or after the player takes his *stance* and is not in a *water hazard*. Snow and natural ice, other than frost, are either *casual water* or *loose impediments*, at the option of the player. Manufactured ice is an *obstruction*. Dew and frost are not *casual water*. A ball is in *casual water* when it lies in or any part of it touches the *casual water*.

Committee The *"Committee"* is the committee in charge of the competition or, if the matter does not arise in a competition, the committee in charge of the *course*.

Competitor A *"competitor"* is a player in a stroke play competition. A *"fellow-competitor"* is any person with whom the competitor plays. Neither is *partner* of the other.

In stroke play *foursome* and *four-ball* competitions, where the context so admits, the word *"competitor"* or *"fellow-competitor"* includes his *partner*.

EQUIPMENT

Equipment includes a golf cart. As it is not being moved by one of the players, the cart and everything in it are deemed to be the equipment of the player whose ball is involved.

GROUND UNDER REPAIR

Course The "*course*" is the whole area within any boundaries established by the *Committee* (see Rule 33-2).

Equipment "*Equipment*" is anything used, worn or carried by or for the player except any ball he has played at the hole being played and any small object, such as a coin or a *tee*, when used to mark the position of a ball or the extent of an area in which a ball is to be dropped. *Equipment* includes a golf cart, whether or not motorised. If such a cart is shared by two or more players, the cart and everything in it are deemed to be the *equipment* of the player whose ball is involved except that, when the cart is being moved by one of the players sharing it, the cart and everything in it are deemed to be that player's *equipment*.
Note: A ball played at the hole being played is *equipment* when it has been lifted and not put back into play.

Fellow-Competitor See "*Competitor*".

Flagstick The "*flagstick*" is a movable straight indicator, with or without bunting or other material attached, centered in the *hole* to show its position. It must be circular in cross-section. Padding or shock absorbent material that might unduly influence the movement of the ball is prohibited.

Forecaddie A "*forecaddie*" is one who is employed by the *Committee* to indicate to players the position of balls during play. He is an *outside agency*.

Four-Ball See "*Matches*".

Foursome See "*Matches*".

Ground Under Repair "*Ground under repair*" is any part of the course so marked by order of the *Committee* or so declared by its authorised representative. It includes material piled for removal and a hole made by a greenkeeper, even if not so marked.
All ground and any grass, bush, tree or other

growing thing within the *ground under repair* is part of the *ground under repair*. The margin of ground under repair extends vertically downwards, but not upwards. Stakes and lines defining *ground under repair* are in such ground. Such stakes are *obstructions*. A ball is in *ground under repair* when it lies in or any part of it touches the *ground under repair*.

Note 1: Grass cuttings and other material left on the *course* that have been abandoned and are not intended to be removed are not *ground under repair* unless so marked.

Note 2: The Committee may make a Local Rule prohibiting play from *ground under repair* or an environmentally-sensitive area defined as *ground under repair*.

Hazards A "*hazard*" is any *bunker* or *water hazard*.

Hole The "*hole*" must be 4¼ inches (108 mm) in diameter and at least 4 inches (101.6 mm)

deep. If a lining is used, it must be sunk at least 1 inch (25.4 mm) below the *putting green* surface unless the nature of the soil makes it impracticable to do so; its outer diameter must not exceed 4¼ inches (108 mm).

Holed A ball is "*holed*" when it is at rest within the circumference of the *hole* and all of it is below the level of the lip of the *hole*.

Honour The player who is to play first from the teeing ground is said to have the "*honour*".

Lateral Water Hazard A "*lateral water hazard*" is a *water hazard* or that part of a *water hazard* so situated that it is not possible or is deemed by the *Committee* to be impracticable to drop a ball behind the *water hazard* in accordance with Rule 26-1b.

That part of a *water hazard* to be played as a *lateral water hazard* should be distinctively marked. A ball is in a *lateral water hazard* when

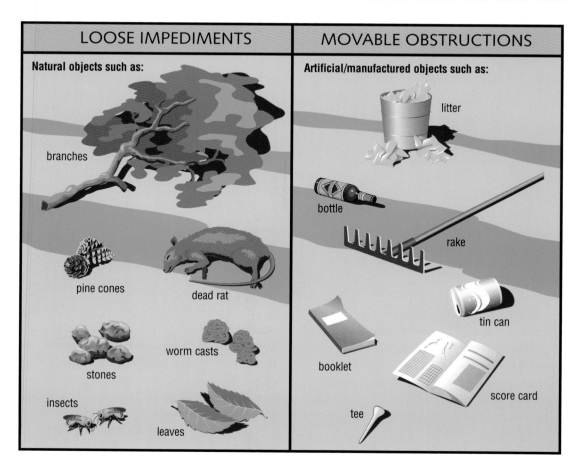

LOOSE IMPEDIMENTS	MOVABLE OBSTRUCTIONS
Natural objects such as:	Artificial/manufactured objects such as:
branches	litter
pine cones	bottle
dead rat	rake
stones	tin can
worm casts	booklet
insects	score card
leaves	tee

it lies in or any part of it touches the *lateral water hazard*.

Note 1: Stakes or lines used to define a *lateral water hazard* must be red. When both stakes and lines are used to define *lateral water hazards*, the stakes identify the *hazard* and the lines define the *hazard* margin.

Note 2: The *Committee* may make a Local Rule prohibiting play from an environmentally-sensitive area defined as a *lateral water hazard*.

Note 3: The *Committee* may define a *lateral water hazard* as a *water hazard*.

Line of Play The *"line of play"* is the direction that the player wishes his ball to take after a *stroke*, plus a reasonable distance on either side of the intended direction. The *line of play* extends vertically upwards from the ground, but does not extend beyond the *hole*.

Line of Putt The *"line of putt"* is the line that the player wishes his ball to take after a *stroke* on the *putting green*. Except with respect to Rule 16-1e, the *line of putt* includes a reasonable distance on either side of the intended line. The *line of putt* does not extend beyond the *hole*.

Loose Impediments *"Loose impediments"* are natural objects, including:
- stones, leaves, twigs, branches and the like,
- dung, and
- worms and insects and the casts and heaps made by them,

provided they are not:
- fixed or growing,
- solidly embedded, or
- adhering to the ball

Sand and loose soil are *loose impediments* on the *putting green*, but not elsewhere.

Snow and natural ice, other than frost, are either *casual water* or *loose impediments* at the option of the player.

Dew and frost are not *loose impediments*.

Lost Ball A ball is deemed *"lost"* if:

a. It is not found or identified as his by the player within five minutes after the player's side or his or their caddies have begun to

BALL DEEMED TO MOVE

This ball is deemed not to have 'moved' because, having left its original position, it rolled back into it again.

This ball is deemed to have 'moved' because it has left its original position and come to rest in another place; the fact that it has moved vertically, rather than laterally, is irrelevant.

search for it; or

b. The player has made a *stroke* at a *substituted ball*; or

c. The player has made a *stroke* at a *provisional ball* from the place where the original ball is likely to be or from a point nearer the *hole* than that place.

Time spent in playing a *wrong ball* is not counted in the five-minute period allowed for search.

Marker A *"marker"* is one who is appointed by the *Committee* to record a *competitor's* score in stroke play. He may be a *fellow-competitor*. He is not a *referee*.

Matches

Single: A match in which one plays against another.

11

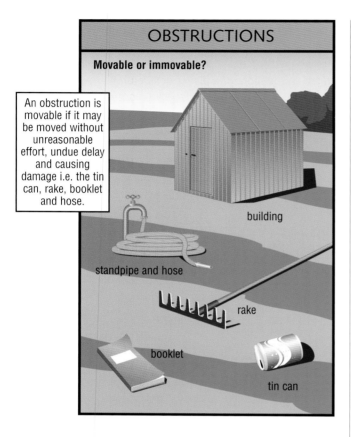

OBSTRUCTIONS

Movable or immovable?

An obstruction is movable if it may be moved without unreasonable effort, undue delay and causing damage i.e. the tin can, rake, booklet and hose.

standpipe and hose

building

rake

booklet

tin can

Threesome: A match in which one plays against two, and each *side* plays one ball.

Foursome: A match in which two play against two, and each *side* plays one ball.

Three-Ball: A match play competition in which three play against one another, each playing his own ball. Each player is playing two distinct matches.

Best-Ball: A match in which one plays against the better ball of two or the best ball of three players.

Four-Ball: A match in which two play their better ball against the better ball of two other players.

Move or Moved A ball is deemed to have "*moved*" if it leaves its position and comes to rest in any other place.

Nearest Point of Relief The "*nearest point of relief*" is the reference point for taking relief without penalty from interference by an immovable *obstruction* (Rule 24-2), an *abnormal ground condition* (Rule 25-1) or a *wrong putting green* (Rule 25-3).

It is the point on the *course* nearest to where the ball lies:

(i) that is not nearer the *hole*, and

(ii) where, if the ball were so positioned, no interference by the condition from which relief is sought would exist for the *stroke* the player would have made from the original position if the condition were not there.

Note: In order to determine the *nearest point of relief* accurately, the player should use the club with which he would have made his next *stroke* if the condition were not there to simulate the *address* position, direction of play and swing for such a *stroke*.

Observer An "*observer*" is one who is appointed by the *Committee* to assist a *referee* to decide questions of fact and to report to him any breach of a *Rule*. An *observer* should not attend the *flagstick*, stand at or mark the position of the *hole*, or lift the ball or mark its position.

Obstructions An "*obstruction*" is anything artificial, including the artificial surfaces and sides of roads and paths and manufactured ice, except:

a. Objects defining *out of bounds*, such as walls, fences, stakes and railings;

b. Any part of an immovable artificial object that is *out of bounds*; and

c. Any construction declared by the *Committee* to be an integral part of the *course*.

An *obstruction* is a movable *obstruction* if it may be moved without unreasonable effort, without unduly delaying play and without causing damage. Otherwise it is an immovable *obstruction*.

Note: The *Committee* may make a Local Rule declaring a movable *obstruction* to be an immovable *obstruction*.

Out of Bounds "*Out of bounds*" is beyond the boundaries of the *course* or any part of the course so marked by the *Committee*.

When *out of bounds* is defined by reference to stakes or a fence or as being beyond stakes or a fence, the *out of bounds* line is determined by the nearest inside points of the stakes or fence posts at ground level excluding angled supports.

PARTNER

A partner is a player associated with another player on the same side.

Objects defining *out of bounds* such as walls, fences, stakes and railings, are not *obstructions* and are deemed to be fixed.

When *out of bounds* is defined by a line on the ground, the line itself is *out of bounds*.

The *out of bounds* line extends vertically upwards and downwards.

A ball is *out of bounds* when all of it lies *out of bounds*.

A player may stand *out of bounds* to play a ball lying within bounds.

Outside Agency An *"outside agency"* is any agency not part of the match or, in stroke play, not part of the *competitor's side*, and includes a *referee*, a *marker*, an *observer* and a *forecaddie*. Neither wind nor water is an *outside agency*.

Partner A *"partner"* is a player associated with another player on the same *side*.

In a *threesome*, *foursome*, *best-ball* or *four-ball* match, where the context so admits, the word player includes his *partner* or *partners*.

Penalty Stroke A *"penalty stroke"* is one added to the score of a player or *side* under certain *Rules*. In a *threesome* or *foursome*, *penalty strokes* do not affect the order of play.

Provisional Ball A *"provisional ball"* is a ball played under Rule 27-2 for a ball that may be *lost* outside a *water hazard* or may be *out of bounds*.

Putting Green The *"putting green"* is all ground of the hole being played that is specially prepared for putting or otherwise defined as such by the *Committee*. A ball is on the *putting green* when any part of it touches the *putting green*.

R&A The *"R&A"* means R&A Rules Limited

Referee A *"referee"* is one who is appointed by the *Committee* to accompany players to decide questions of fact and apply the *Rules*. He must act on any breach of a *Rule* that he observes or is reported to him.

A *referee* should not attend the *flagstick*, stand at or mark the position of the *hole*, or lift the ball or mark its position.

Rub of the Green A *"rub of the green"* occurs when a ball in motion is accidentally deflected or stopped by any *outside agency* (see Rule 19-1).

Rule or Rules The term *"Rule"* includes:
a. The Rules of Golf and their interpretations as contained in Decisions on the Rules of Golf;
b. Any Conditions of Competition established by the *Committee* under Rule 33-1 and Appendix I;
c. Any Local Rules established by the *Committee* under Rule 33-8a and Appendix I; and
d. The specifications on clubs and the ball in Appendices II and III.

Side
A "side" is a player, or two or more players who are *partners*.

13

Single See *"Matches"*.

Stance Taking the *"stance"* consists in a player placing his feet in position for and preparatory to making a *stroke*.

Stipulated Round The *"stipulated round"* consists of playing the holes of the *course* in their correct sequence unless otherwise authorised by the *Committee*. The number of holes in a *stipulated round* is 18 unless a smaller number is authorised by the *Committee*. As to extension of *stipulated round* in match play, see Rule 2-3.

Stroke A *"stroke"* is the forward movement of the club made with the intention of striking at and moving the ball, but if a player checks his downswing voluntarily before the clubhead reaches the ball he has not made a *stroke*.

Substituted Ball A *"substituted ball"* is a ball put into play for the original ball that was either *in play, lost, out of bounds* or lifted.

Tee A *"tee"* is a device designed to raise the ball off the ground. It must not be longer than 4 inches (101.6 mm) and it must not be designed or manufactured in such a way that it could indicate the *line of play* or influence the movement of the ball.

Teeing Ground The *"teeing ground"* is the starting place for the hole to be played. It is a rectangular area two club-lengths in depth, the front and the sides of which are defined by the outside limits of two tee-markers. A ball is outside the *teeing ground* when all of it lies outside the *teeing ground*.

Three-Ball See *"Matches"*.

Threesomes See *"Matches"*.

Through the Green *"Through the green"* is the whole area of the course except:
a. The *teeing ground* and *putting green* of the

hole being played; and
b. All *hazards* on the *course*.

Water Hazard A *"water hazard"* is any sea, lake, pond, river, ditch, surface drainage ditch or other open water course (whether or not containing water) and anything of a similar nature on the *course*.

  All ground or water within the margin of a *water hazard* is part of the *water hazard*. The margin of a *water hazard* extends vertically upwards and downwards. Stakes and lines defining the margins of *water hazards* are in the *hazards*. Such stakes are *obstructions*. A ball is in a *water hazard* when it lies in or any part of it touches the *water hazard*.
Note 1: Stakes or lines used to define a *water hazard* must be yellow. When both stakes and lines are used to define *water hazards*, the stakes identify the *hazard* and the lines define the *hazard* margin.
Note 2: The *Committee* may make a Local Rule prohibiting play from an environmentally-sensitive area defined as a *water hazard*.

Wrong Ball A *"wrong ball"* is any ball other than the player's:
• *ball in play*;
• *provisional ball*; or
• second ball played under Rule 3-3 or Rule 20-7c in stroke play; and includes
• another player's ball;
• an abandoned ball; and
• the player's original ball when it is no longer *in play*
Note: *Ball in play* includes a ball *substituted* for the *ball in play*, whether or not the substitution is permitted.

Wrong Putting Green A *"wrong putting green"* is any *putting green* other than that of the hole being played. Unless otherwise prescribed by the *Committee*, this term includes a practice *putting green* or pitching green on the *course*.

DEFINITION OF A STROKE

At this point, as the player has not started his downswing, he has not begun his stroke. Once the player begins his downswing he is considered to have made a stroke, unless he checks his downswing voluntarily.

TEEING GROUND

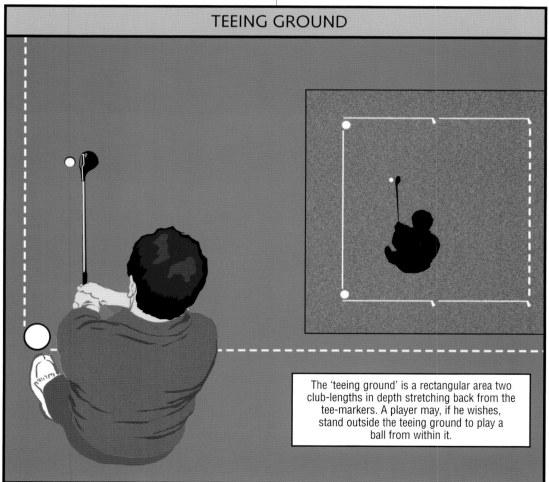

The 'teeing ground' is a rectangular area two club-lengths in depth stretching back from the tee-markers. A player may, if he wishes, stand outside the teeing ground to play a ball from within it.

SECTION 3
THE RULES OF PLAY

RULE **1** | ## THE GAME

DEFINITIONS

All defined terms are in *italics* and are listed alphabetically in the Definitions section – see pages 6–15.

1-1. GENERAL
The Game of Golf consists of playing a ball with a club from the *teeing ground* into the *hole* by a *stroke* or successive *strokes* in accordance with the *Rules*.

1-2. EXERTING INFLUENCE ON BALL
A player or *caddie* must not take any action to influence the position or the movement of a ball except in accordance with the *Rules*.
(Removal of movable obstruction – see Rule 24-1)

PENALTY FOR BREACH OF RULE 1-2:

Match play – Loss of hole; Stroke play – Two strokes.

Note: In the case of a serious breach of Rule 1-2, the *Committee* may impose a penalty of disqualification.

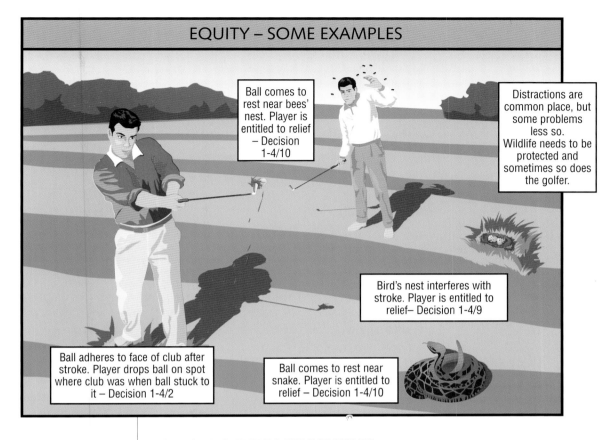

EQUITY – SOME EXAMPLES

Ball comes to rest near bees' nest. Player is entitled to relief – Decision 1-4/10

Distractions are common place, but some problems less so. Wildlife needs to be protected and sometimes so does the golfer.

Bird's nest interferes with stroke. Player is entitled to relief– Decision 1-4/9

Ball adheres to face of club after stroke. Player drops ball on spot where club was when ball stuck to it – Decision 1-4/2

Ball comes to rest near snake. Player is entitled to relief – Decision 1-4/10

1-3. AGREEMENT TO WAIVE RULES

Players must not agree to exclude the operation of any *Rule* or to waive any penalty incurred.

PENALTY FOR BREACH OF RULE 1-3:
Match play – Disqualification of both sides;
Stroke play – Disqualification of competitors concerned.

(Agreeing to play out of turn in stroke play – see Rule 10-2c)

See **incident** involving Rule 1-4 below

1-4. POINTS NOT COVERED BY RULES

If any point in dispute is not covered by the *Rules*, the decision should be made in accordance with equity.

RULE 1 INCIDENT

During the 1990 Dunhill Cup at St. Andrews, on the 17th hole of the final, Mark James hit his second stroke onto the road behind the green. Philip Walton, James's fellow-competitor, hit his approach into the famous Road Hole bunker.

While James was preparing for his third stroke from the road, Walton stepped into the bunker to assess his next stroke. Due to the nature of the stroke from the road, James felt it was possible that he might over hit his third stroke. The likely result being that the ball would finish in the bunker, he was concerned that the footprints made

17

by Walton in the bunker may have an adverse effect on his lie.

At this point James sought clarification from a Rules official as to whether he could have Walton's footprints raked. The referee ruled, in equity (Rule 1-4), that James could have the bunker raked, thereby restoring it to its former condition as the footprints had been created by Walton after James's ball had come to rest on the road. As a result of this incident, Decision 13-2/29.5 was introduced in the *Decisions on the Rules of Golf*.

RULE 2 | MATCH PLAY

DEFINITIONS

All defined terms are in *italics* and are listed alphabetically in the Definitions section – see pages 6–15.

2-1. GENERAL

A match consists of *one side* playing against another over a *stipulated round* unless otherwise decreed by the *Committee*.

In match play the game is played by holes.

Except as otherwise provided in the *Rules*, a hole is won by the *side* that *holes* its ball in the fewer *strokes*. In a handicap match the lower net score wins the hole.

The state of the match is expressed by the terms: so many "holes up" or "all square" and so many "to play".

A *side* is "dormie" when it is as many holes up as there are holes remaining to be played.

2-2. HALVED HOLE

A hole is halved if each *side holes* out in the same number of *strokes*. When a player has *holed* out and his opponent has been left with a *stroke* for the half, if the player subsequently incurs a penalty, the hole is halved.

2-3. WINNER OF MATCH

A match is won when one *side* leads by a number of holes greater than the number remaining to be played.

If there is a tie, the *Committee* may extend the *stipulated round* by as many holes as are required for a match to be won.

2-4. CONCESSION OF NEXT STROKE, HOLE OR MATCH

A player may concede his opponent's next *stroke* at any time provided the opponent's ball is at rest. The opponent is considered to have *holed* out with his next *stroke* and the ball may be removed by either *side*.

A player may concede a hole at any time prior to the start or conclusion of that hole.

A player may concede a match at any time prior to the start or conclusion of that match.

A concession may not be declined or withdrawn.

(Ball overhanging hole – see Rule 16-2)

See **incident** involving Rule 2-4 on page 20–21

WINNER OF MATCH: HOLE-BY-HOLE PLAY-OFF

2-5. DOUBT AS TO PROCEDURE; DISPUTES AND CLAIMS

In match play, if a doubt or dispute arises between the players, a player may make a claim. If no duly authorised representative of the *Committee* is available within a reasonable time, the players must continue the match without delay. The *Committee* may consider a claim only if the player making the claim notifies his opponent (i) that he is making a claim, (ii) of the facts of the situation and (iii) that he wants a ruling. The claim must be made before any player in the match plays from the next *teeing ground* or, in the case of the last hole of the match, before all players in the match leave the *putting green*.

A later claim may not be considered by the *Committee* unless it is based on facts previously unknown to the player making the claim and he had been given wrong information (Rules 6-2a and 9) by an opponent.

Once the result of the match has been officially announced, a later claim may not be considered by the *Committee* unless it is satisfied that the opponent knew he was giving wrong information.

STATUS OF LATE CLAIM

I've just realised that my opponent should have lost the 4th when he grounded his club in the bunker.

I'm afraid such a claim had to be made before you or your opponent played from the 5th tee. The Committee can only consider a later claim if the facts were previously unknown to you.

2-6. GENERAL PENALTY

The penalty for a breach of a *Rule* in match play is loss of hole except when otherwise provided.

RULE 2 INCIDENT

Jack Nicklaus' concession of Tony Jacklin's putt on the final hole during the final match of the 1969 Ryder Cup resulted in the event's first tie, and is hailed as one of golf's finest acts of sportsmanship.

Going into the final day's competition at Royal Birkdale Golf Club in Southport, England, the United States and Great Britain and Ireland were even at eight points apiece. That morning's singles matches resulted in a two-point lead for Great Britain and Ireland but the U.S. responded in the afternoon to leave the matches tied at 15 points each with only the final match of Nicklaus and Jacklin still on the course. Eighteen of the 32 Ryder Cup matches went to the final hole that year, and it was there that the three-day competition would be ultimately decided.

Nicklaus seemed to have the upper hand as Jacklin fell behind on the back nine but the reigning Open champion Jacklin, would not relent. Indeed, he eagled the 17th to go all square with Nicklaus.

At the par-5 18th, Jacklin missed his putt for birdie. Nicklaus holed his four-footer for par leaving Jacklin with a short putt to tie Nicklaus. If he holed the putt it would be a tie but a miss by Jacklin would result in an outright win by the Americans.

Before Jacklin could putt, Nicklaus conceded the Englishman's putt

Tony Jacklin and Jack Nicklaus shake hands on the 18th green during the 1969 Ryder Cup.

thereby ensuring a tie. "I don't think you would have missed that Tony," Nicklaus reportedly said, "but under these circumstances I'd never give you the opportunity."

"The length of the putt has varied after thirty years," Jacklin has stated recently to reporters. "It's been as long as four feet. But my recollection is twenty inches. Of course, I could have missed it; there are no guarantees in golf, especially in the crucible of the Ryder Cup, but I believe I would have made it. But Jack saw the big picture, two months before I had become the first British player in 18 years to win the Open, so there was very much a pro-British fervour at the Ryder Cup in England that year. Jack saw that the putt on the last hole in 1969 meant a heck of a lot more to the Ryder Cup than who won or lost that particular match. It was a great moment."

21

RULE **3** | # STROKE PLAY

DEFINITIONS All defined terms are in *italics* and are listed alphabetically in the Definitions section – see pages 6–15.

3-1. WINNER

The *competitor* who plays the *stipulated round* or rounds in the fewest *strokes* is the winner.

In a handicap competition, the *competitor* with the lowest net score for the *stipulated round* or rounds is the winner.

3-2. FAILURE TO HOLE OUT

See **incident** concerning Rule 3-2 on page 23

If a *competitor* fails to hole out at any hole and does not correct his mistake before he makes a *stroke* on the next *teeing ground* or, in the case of the last hole of the round, before he leaves the *putting green*, **he is disqualified**.

3-3. DOUBT AS TO PROCEDURE
a. Procedure

In stroke play, if a *competitor* is doubtful of his rights or the correct procedure during play of a hole he may, without penalty, complete the hole with two balls.

After the doubtful situation has arisen and before taking further action, the *competitor* must announce to his *marker* or a *fellow-competitor* that he intends to play two balls and which ball he wishes to count if the *Rules* permit. If he fails to do so, the provisions of Rule 3-3b(ii) apply.

The *competitor* must report the facts of the situation to the Committee before returning his score card. If he fails to do so, **he is disqualified**.

b. Determination of Score for Hole

(i)   If the ball that the *competitor* selected in advance to count has been played in accordance with the *Rules*, the score with that ball is the *competitor's* score for the hole. Otherwise, the score with the other ball counts if the *Rules* allow the procedure adopted for that ball.

(ii)   If the *competitor* fails to announce in advance his decision to complete the hole with two balls, or which ball he wishes to count, the score with the original ball counts, provided it has been played in accordance with the *Rules*. If the original ball is not one of the balls being played, the first ball put into play counts, provided it has been played in accordance with the *Rules*. Otherwise, the score with the other ball counts if the *Rules* allow the procedure adopted for that ball.

Note 1: If a *competitor* plays a second ball under Rule 3-3, the *strokes* made after this Rule has been invoked with the ball ruled not to count and *penalty strokes* incurred solely by playing that ball are disregarded.

Note 2: A second ball played under Rule 3-3 is not a *provisional ball* under Rule 27-2.

3-4. REFUSAL TO COMPLY WITH A RULE

If a *competitor* refuses to comply with a *Rule* affecting the rights of another *competitor*, **he is disqualified**.

3-5. GENERAL PENALTY

The penalty for a breach of a *Rule* in stroke play is two strokes except when otherwise provided.

RULE 3 INCIDENT

In the 1997 Volvo PGA Championship at Wentworth, on the 13th hole, Nick Faldo chipped his ball from just off the green, the ball coming to rest against the flagstick. At this time the ball was not holed as all of the ball was not below the level of the lip of the hole.

While Faldo acknowledged the applause of the crowd and passed his club back to his caddie, his fellow-competitor, Ernie Els, walked to the hole, lifted Faldo's ball and returned it to him. The incident was televised and a number of viewers telephoned the Tournament Office concerned that Faldo's ball may not have been holed before Els picked it up.

The incident was reviewed by officials as Faldo completed his round and it transpired that, off camera, the ball had fallen into the hole before Els lifted it from the hole and therefore there was no question of Faldo having breached Rule 3-2 for failing to hole out.

The *R&A* reserves the right, at any time, to change the Rules relating to clubs and balls (see Appendices II and III) and make or change the interpretations relating to these Rules.

RULE CLUBS

A player in doubt as to the conformity of a club should consult the *R&A*. A manufacturer should submit to the *R&A* a sample of a club to be manufactured for a ruling as to whether the club conforms with the *Rules*. If a manufacturer fails to submit a sample or to await a ruling before manufacturing and/or marketing the club, the manufacturer assumes the risk of a ruling that the club does not conform with the *Rules*. Any sample submitted to the *R&A* becomes its property for reference purposes.

DEFINITIONS

All defined terms are in *italics* and are listed alphabetically in the Definitions section – see pages 6–15.

4-1. FORM AND MAKE OF CLUBS
a. General
The player's clubs must conform with this Rule and the provisions, specifications and interpretations set forth in Appendix II.

b. Wear and Alteration
A club that conforms with the *Rules* when new is deemed to conform after wear through normal use. Any part of a club that has been purposely altered is regarded as new and must, in its altered state, conform with the *Rules*.

4-2. PLAYING CHARACTERISTICS CHANGED AND FOREIGN MATERIAL
a. Playing Characteristics Changed
During a *stipulated round*, the playing characteristics of a club must not be purposely changed by adjustment or by any other means.

b. Foreign Material
Foreign material must not be applied to the club face for the purpose of influencing the movement of the ball.

PENALTY FOR BREACH OF RULE 4-1 or 4-2:
Disqualification.

4-3. DAMAGED CLUBS: REPAIR AND REPLACEMENT
a. Damage in Normal Course of Play
If, during a *stipulated round*, a player's club is damaged in the normal course of play, he may:
(i) use the club in its damaged state for the remainder of the *stipulated round*; or

(ii) without unduly delaying play, repair it or have it repaired; or

(iii) as an additional option available only if the club is unfit for play, replace the damaged club with any club. The replacement of a club must not unduly delay play and must not be made by borrowing any club selected for play by any other person playing on the *course*.

PENALTY FOR BREACH OF RULE 4-3a:
See Penalty Statement for Rule 4-4a or b, and c.

Note: A club is unfit for play if it is substantially damaged, e.g., the shaft is dented, significantly bent or breaks into pieces; the clubhead becomes loose, detached or significantly deformed; or the grip becomes loose. A club is not unfit for play solely because the club's lie or loft has been altered, or the clubhead is scratched.

See **incident** involving Rule 4-3b on page 27

b. Damage Other Than in Normal Course of Play

If, during a *stipulated round*, a player's club is damaged other than in the normal course of play rendering it non-conforming or changing its playing characteristics, the club must not subsequently be used or replaced during the round.

c. Damage Prior to Round

A player may use a club damaged prior to a round provided the club, in its damaged state, conforms with the *Rules*.

Damage to a club that occurred prior to a round may be repaired during the round, provided the playing characteristics are not changed and play is not unduly delayed.

PENALTY FOR BREACH OF RULE 4-3b or c:
Disqualification.

(Undue delay – see Rule 6-7)

CLUB UNFIT FOR PLAY

If a player's club is damaged in the normal course of play (e.g. in playing a stroke or in taking a practice swing) rendering it unfit for play, the player may, without unduly delaying play, repair it or have it repaired or replace the damaged club with any club. However, he may not borrow a club being used by anyone playing on the course.

When a club is damaged other than in the normal course of play it may not be used during the remainder of the round. Ben Crenshaw became more familiar with the provisions of Rule 4-3b at the 1987 Ryder Cup match. See the story on page 27.

4-4. MAXIMUM OF FOURTEEN CLUBS
a. Selection and Addition of Clubs

The player must not start a *stipulated round* with more than fourteen clubs. He is limited to the clubs **thus selected** for that round except that, if he started with fewer than **fourteen clubs**, he may add any number provided his total number does not **exceed fourteen.**

The addition of a club or clubs must not unduly delay play (Rule 6-7) and the player must not **add or borrow** any club selected for play by any other person playing on the *course.*

b. Partners May Share Clubs

Partners may share clubs, provided that the total number of clubs carried by the *partners* so sharing does not exceed fourteen.

PENALTY FOR BREACH OF RULE 4-4a or b,
REGARDLESS OF NUMBER OF EXCESS CLUBS CARRIED:

Match play – At the conclusion of the hole at which the breach is discovered, the state of the match is adjusted by deducting one hole for each hole at which a breach occurred. Maximum deduction per round: Two holes.

Stroke play – Two strokes for each hole at which any breach occurred; maximum penalty per round: Four strokes.

Bogey and par competitions – Penalties as in match play.

Stableford competitions – see Note 1 to Rule 32-1b.

c. Excess Club Declared Out of Play

Any club or clubs carried or used in breach of Rule 4-3a(iii) or Rule 4-4 must be declared out of play by the player to his opponent in match play or his *marker* or a *fellow-competitor* in stroke play immediately upon discovery that a breach has occurred. The player must not use the club or clubs for the remainder of the *stipulated round.*

PENALTY FOR BREACH OF RULE 4-4c:
Disqualification.

RULE 4 INCIDENT

As Ben Crenshaw walked down a gravel pathway at Muirfield Village during the 1987 Ryder Cup, he was bouncing his putter along the ground in time with his steps when the club's shaft broke.

It was the third and final day of the competition and Crenshaw was competing against Eamonn Darcy in the singles. The American team had finished the previous day trailing the European team by five points. The matches in front of Crenshaw and Darcy were tilting in favour of the Americans, and those behind could go either way so every point had become crucial.

It did not matter that Crenshaw's putter was damaged without anger or malice. Because the club was damaged other than in the normal course of play, America's best putter would now suffer the consequences of Rule 4. He could not use the putter, repair or replace it.

For the remainder of the match Crenshaw used various clubs for putting – sometimes a 1-iron, sometimes a sand wedge. The Texan's misfortune, coupled with the intensity of the Ryder Cup singles competition, seemed to provide extraordinary focus and he continued to putt well, especially well since he didn't have a putter. The match went to the 18th hole where Darcy won 1 up.

With a final score of 15-13, the European team won the Ryder Cup for the first time on American soil.

RULE | # THE BALL

DEFINITIONS

All defined terms are in *italics* and are listed alphabetically in the Definitions section – see pages 6–15.

5-1. GENERAL
The ball the player plays must conform to requirements specified in Appendix III.
Note: The *Committee* may require, in the conditions of a competition (Rule 33-1), that the ball the player plays must be named on the current List of Conforming Golf Balls issued by the *R&A*.

5-2. FOREIGN MATERIAL
Foreign material must not be applied to a ball for the purpose of changing its playing characteristics.

PENALTY FOR BREACH OF RULE 5-1 or 5-2:

Disqualification.

5-3. BALL UNFIT FOR PLAY
A ball is unfit for play if it is visibly cut, cracked or out of shape. A ball is not unfit for play solely because mud or other materials adhere to it, its surface is scratched or scraped or its paint is damaged or discoloured.

If a player has reason to believe his ball has become unfit for play during play of the hole being played, he may lift the ball without penalty to

See **incident** involving Rule 5-3 on page 30

27

determine whether it is unfit.

Before lifting the ball, the player must announce his intention to his opponent in match play or his *marker* or a *fellow-competitor* in stroke play and mark the position of the ball. He may then lift and examine it provided that he gives his opponent, *marker* or *fellow-competitor* an opportunity to examine the ball and observe the lifting and replacement. The ball must not be cleaned when lifted under Rule 5-3. If the player fails to comply with all or any part of this procedure, **he incurs a penalty of one stroke.**

If it is determined that the ball has become unfit for play during play of the hole being played, the player may *substitute* another ball, placing it on the spot where the original ball lay. Otherwise, the original ball must be replaced. If a player *substitutes* a ball when not permitted and he makes a *stroke* at the wrongly *substituted* ball, **he incurs the general penalty for a breach of Rule 5-3**, but there is no additional penalty under this Rule or Rule 15-1.

If a ball breaks into pieces as a result of a *stroke*, the *stroke* is cancelled and the player must play a ball without penalty as nearly as possible at the spot from which the original ball was played (see Rule 20-5).

PENALTY FOR BREACH OF RULE 5-3:

Match play – Loss of hole; Stroke play – Two strokes.

*If a player incurs the general penalty for a breach of Rule 5-3, there is no additional penalty under this Rule.

Note: If the opponent, *marker* or *fellow-competitor* wishes to dispute a claim of unfitness, he must do so before the player plays another ball.
(Cleaning ball lifted from putting green or under any other Rule – see Rule 21)

The player must give his opponent, marker or fellow-competitor an opportunity to inspect a ball that a player believes is unfit for play. In some cases, a referee may be asked to participate in this process. See the story on page 30 involving Tiger Woods at the 1994 U.S. Amateur.

RULE 5 INCIDENT

On the 32nd hole of the final of the 1994 U.S. Amateur Championship, Tiger Woods learned that one of the very specific instances in the Rules when a referee is not to be involved, except as a last resort, is in determining whether or not a ball is unfit for play during the play of a hole.

One down to Trip Kuehne with five holes left in the 36-hole match, Woods' drive from the 14th tee of the TPC at Sawgrass struck a cart path and a media vehicle before finally coming to rest.

Having played his second shot on to the putting green, Woods marked and lifted his ball. It was then that he questioned whether or not his ball had been rendered unfit for play by virtue of its striking the path and the vehicle. Woods' inquiry was directed to the referee who was walking with the match. The referee responded that Woods would have to make that determination after giving his opponent an opportunity to examine the ball.

After inspecting Woods' ball, Kuehne said he was unsure whether or not it was unfit. This sent Woods back to the referee for an opinion.

While Decision 5-3/7 permits a referee to make such a decision, it also states that every effort should be made to have the opponent, marker or fellow-competitor fulfill his responsibilities under Rule 5-3. In this situation, Woods' opponent was not able to fulfill his responsibilities because he did not know if a ball was unfit simply because it was scarred from bouncing off a cart path.

With Kuehne unsure and Woods entitled to a ruling, the referee determined that a new ball could not be substituted. Rule 5-3 is specific in stating that a ball is not unfit when its surface is scratched or scraped or its paint is damaged or discoloured.

Woods halved the hole with the scraped ball. After birdies at the 16th and 17th, Woods was 1 up. Woods' par, at the 18th, gave him a 2 up victory and the first of his three consecutive U.S. Amateur titles.

RULE THE PLAYER

DEFINITIONS

All defined terms are in *italics* and are listed alphabetically in the Definitions section – see pages 6–15.

6-1. RULES

The player and his *caddie* are responsible for knowing the *Rules*. During a *stipulated round*, for any breach of a *Rule* by his *caddie*, the player incurs the applicable penalty.

6-2. HANDICAP
a. Match Play

Before starting a match in a handicap competition, the players should determine from one another their respective handicaps. If a player begins a match having declared a handicap higher than that to which he is entitled and this affects the number of strokes given or received, **he is disqualified**; otherwise, the player must play off the declared handicap.

b. Stroke Play

In any round of a handicap competition, the *competitor* must ensure that his handicap is recorded on his score card before it is returned to the *Committee*. If no handicap is recorded on his score card before it is returned (Rule 6-6b), or if the recorded handicap is higher than that to which he is entitled and this affects the number of strokes received, **he is disqualified** from the handicap competition; otherwise, the score stands.

Note: It is the player's responsibility to know the holes at which handicap strokes are to be given or received.

6-3. TIME OF STARTING AND GROUPS
a. Time of Starting

The player must start at the time established by the *Committee*.

b. Groups

In stroke play, the *competitor* must remain throughout the round in the group arranged by the *Committee* unless the *Committee* authorises or ratifies a change.

PENALTY FOR BREACH OF RULE 6-3:
Disqualification.

(Best-ball and four-ball play – see Rules 30-3a and 31-2)

Note: The *Committee* may provide in the conditions of a competition (Rule 33-1) that, if the player arrives at his starting point, ready to play, within five minutes after his starting time, in the absence of circumstances that warrant waiving the penalty of disqualification as provided in Rule 33-7, the penalty for failure to start on time is **loss of the first hole in match play or two strokes at the first hole in stroke play instead of disqualification.**

6-4. CADDIE

The player may be assisted by a *caddie*, but he is limited to only one *caddie* at any one time.

PENALTY FOR BREACH OF RULE 6-4:
Match play – At the conclusion of the hole at which the breach is discovered, the state of the match is adjusted by deducting one hole for each hole at which a breach occurred; maximum deduction per round – Two holes.
Stroke play – Two strokes for each hole at which any breach occurred; maximum penalty per round – Four strokes.
Match or stroke play – In the event of a breach between the play of two holes, the penalty applies to the next hole.
A player having more than one caddie in breach of this Rule must immediately upon discovery that a breach has occurred ensure that he has no more than one caddie at any one time during the remainder of the stipulated round. Otherwise, the player is disqualified.
Bogey and par competitions – Penalties as in match play.
Stableford competitions – see Note 2 to Rule 32-1b

Note: The *Committee* may, in the conditions of a competition (Rule 33-1), prohibit the use of *caddies* or restrict a player in his choice of *caddie*.

The responsibility for playing the proper ball rests with the player. PGA Tour player Duffy Waldorf has his wife and children assist him in putting identification marks on his golf balls.

6-5. BALL
The responsibility for playing the proper ball rests with the player. Each player should put an identification mark on his ball.

6-6. SCORING IN STROKE PLAY
a. Recording Scores
After each hole the *marker* should check the score with the *competitor* and record it. On completion of the round the *marker* must sign the score card and hand it to the *competitor*. If more than one *marker* records the scores, each must sign for the part for which he is responsible.

b. Signing and Returning Score Card

See **incident** involving Rule 6-6b on page 37–38

After completion of the round, the *competitor* should check his score for each hole and settle any doubtful points with the *Committee*. He must ensure that the *marker* or *markers* have signed the score card, sign the score card himself and return it to the *Committee* as soon as possible.

PENALTY FOR BREACH OF RULE 6-6b:
Disqualification.

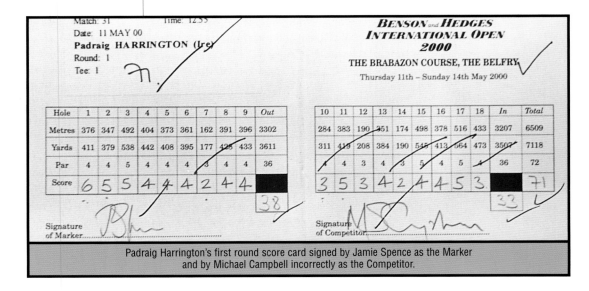

Padraig Harrington's first round score card signed by Jamie Spence as the Marker and by Michael Campbell incorrectly as the Competitor.

SCORING IN STROKE PLAY

COMPETITION **SPRING STROKE PLAY**   DATE **14 . 6 . 95**

PLAYER **D. BROWN**   HANDICAP **10**   Game No **21**

Hole	Yards	Par	Stroke Index	Score	W=• L=• H=0 POINTS	Mar Score	Hole	Yards	Par	Stroke Index	Score	W=• L=• H=0 POINTS	Mar Score
1	312	4	17	5		6	10	369	4	12	6 5 **c**		
2	446	4	1	4		4	11	433	4	2	3		
3	310	4	13	4		3	12	361	4	14	4		
4	370	4	9	5	**b**	5	13	415	4	6	5		
5	478	5	3	6			14	155	3	16	6		
8 7	429	4	11	4			15	338	4	8	5		
7 6	385	4	5	3			16	316	4	10	4		
8	178	3	7	4			17	191	3	4	5		
9	354	4	15	6			18	508	5	18	7		
OUT	3262			41			IN	3086	35		44		
							OUT	3262	36		41		
							TOTAL	6348	71		85		

a

Markers Signature **D.B.** **e & f**

Players Signature **Bill White**

HANDICAP **10** **d**
NETT **75**

Competitor's Responsibilities:

1. To record the correct handicap somewhere on the score card before it is returned to the Committee.
2. To check the gross score recorded for each hole is correct.
3. To ensure that the marker has signed the card and to countersign the card himself before it is returned to the Committee.

Committee Responsibilities:

1. Issue to each competitor a score card containing the date and the competitor's name.
2. To add the scores for each hole and apply the handicap recorded on the card.

(**a**) Hole numbers may be altered if hole scores have been recorded in the wrong boxes.
(**b**) A marker need not keep a record of his own score, however it is recommended.
(**c**) There is nothing in the Rules that requires an alteration to be initialled.
(**d**) The competitor is responsible only for the correctness of the score recorded for each hole. If the competitor records a wrong total score or net score, the Committee must correct the error, without penalty to the competitor. In this instance, the Committee have added the scores for each hole and applied the handicap.
(**e**) There is no penalty if a marker signs the competitor's score card in the space provided for the competitor's signature, and the competitor then signs in the space provided for the marker's signature.
(**f**) The initialing of the score card by the competitor is sufficient for the purpose of countersignature.

c. Alteration of Score Card

No alteration may be made on a score card after the *competitor* has returned it to the *Committee*.

d. Wrong Score for Hole

See **incident** involving Rule 6-6d on page 37–38

The *competitor* is responsible for the correctness of the score recorded for each hole on his score card. If he returns a score for any hole lower than actually taken, **he is disqualified**. If he returns a score for any hole higher than actually taken, the score as returned stands.

Note 1: The *Committee* is responsible for the addition of scores and application of the handicap recorded on the score card – see Rule 33-5.

Note 2: In *four-ball* stroke play, see also Rule 31-4 and -7a.

6-7. UNDUE DELAY; SLOW PLAY

The player must play without undue delay and in accordance with any pace of play guidelines that the *Committee* may establish. Between completion of a hole and playing from the next *teeing ground*, the player must not unduly delay play.

PENALTY FOR BREACH OF RULE 6-7:

Match play – Loss of hole; Stroke play – Two strokes
Bogey and par competitions – See Note 3 to Rule 32-1a.
Stableford competitions – See Note 3 to Rule 32-1b.
For subsequent offence – Disqualification.

Note 1: If the player unduly delays play between holes, he is delaying the play of the next hole and, except for bogey, par and Stableford competitions (see Rule 32), the penalty applies to that hole.

Note 2: For the purpose of preventing slow play, the *Committee* may, in the conditions of a competition (Rule 33-1), establish pace of play guidelines

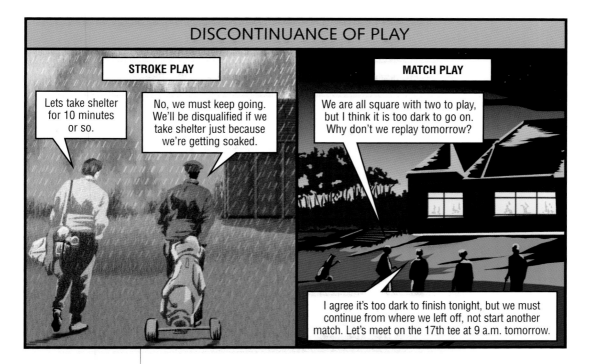

including maximum periods of time allowed to complete a *stipulated round*, a hole or a *stroke*.

In stroke play only, the *Committee* may, in such a condition, modify the penalty for a breach of this Rule as follows:

First offence – One stroke

Second offence – Two strokes

For subsequent offence – Disqualification.

6-8. DISCONTINUANCE OF PLAY; RESUMPTION OF PLAY
a. When Permitted

The player must not discontinue play unless:

(i)   the *Committee* has suspended play;

(ii)   he believes there is danger from lightning;

(iii)   he is seeking a decision from the *Committee* on a doubtful or disputed point (see Rules 2-5 and 34-3); or

(iv)   there is some other good reason such as sudden illness.

Bad weather is not of itself a good reason for discontinuing play.

If the player discontinues play without specific permission from the *Committee*, he must report to the *Committee* as soon as practicable. If he does so and the *Committee* considers his reason satisfactory, there is no penalty. Otherwise, **the player is disqualified**.

Exception in match play: Players discontinuing match play by agreement are not subject to disqualification unless by so doing the competition is delayed.

Note: Leaving the course does not of itself constitute discontinuance of play.

b. Procedure When Play Suspended by Committee

When play is suspended by the *Committee*, if the players in a match or group are between the play of two holes, they must not resume play until the *Committee* has ordered a resumption of play. If they have started play of a hole, they may discontinue play immediately or continue play of the hole, provided they do so without delay. If the players choose to continue play of the hole, they are permitted to discontinue play before completing it. In any case, play must be discontinued after the hole is completed.

The players must resume play when the *Committee* has ordered a resumption of play.

PENALTY FOR BREACH OF RULE 6-8b:
Disqualification.

Note: The *Committee* may provide in the conditions of a competition (Rule 33-1) that, in potentially dangerous situations, play must be discontinued immediately following a suspension of play by the *Committee*. If a player fails to discontinue play immediately, **he is disqualified** unless circumstances warrant waiving the penalty as provided in Rule 33-7.

c. Lifting Ball When Play Discontinued

When a player discontinues play of a hole under Rule 6-8a, he may lift his ball without penalty only if the *Committee* has suspended play or there is a good reason to lift it. Before lifting the ball the player must mark its position. If the player discontinues play and lifts his ball without specific permission from the *Committee*, he must, when reporting to the *Committee* (Rule 6-8a), report the lifting of the ball.

If the player lifts the ball without a good reason to do so, fails to mark the position of the ball before lifting it or fails to report the lifting of the ball, **he incurs a penalty of one stroke**.

d. Procedure When Play Resumed

Play must be resumed from where it was discontinued, even if resumption occurs on a subsequent day. The player must, either before or when play is resumed, proceed as follows:

(i)   if the player has lifted the ball, he must, provided he was entitled to lift it under Rule 6-8c, place a ball on the spot from which the original ball was lifted. Otherwise, the original ball must be placed on the spot from which it was lifted;

(ii) if the player entitled to lift his ball under Rule 6-8c has not done so, he may lift, clean and replace the ball, or *substitute* a ball on the spot from which the original ball was lifted. Before lifting the ball he must mark its position; or

(iii) if the player's ball or ball-marker is moved (including by wind or water) while play is discontinued, a ball or ball-marker must be placed on the spot from which the original ball or ball-marker was moved.

Note: If the spot where the ball is to be placed is impossible to determine, it must be estimated and the ball placed on the estimated spot. The provisions of Rule 20-3c do not apply.

***PENALTY FOR BREACH OF RULE 6-8c or d:**
Match play – Loss of hole; Stroke play – Two strokes.

***If a player incurs the general penalty for a breach of Rule 6-8d, there is no additional penalty under Rule 6-8c.**

A solemn Padraig Harrington following his final day disqualification from the 2000 Benson & Hedges International for failing to sign his first round score card.

RULE 6 INCIDENTS

As the ultimate testament to a player's performance on the course in a stroke play competition, the score card must never contain a score lower than actually taken and it must be signed by the competitor, attested by the marker and returned as soon as possible to the Committee. Failure to meet any of these criteria results in disqualification.

Roberto De Vicenzo signed for a higher score than he actually made at the 1968 Masters Tournament, which did not disqualify him but it kept the Argentinean from forcing a play-off with Bob Goalby.

Playing in front of Goalby on Sunday, De Vicenzo, the reigning Open Champion, sank a five-foot birdie putt on the 17th hole for a 3. A bogey at the 18th gave him an 11-under total of 277. Goalby managed a five-footer for par at the 18th for a 66 and another 277.

However, De Vicenzo's fellow-competitor and marker, Tommy Aaron, had mistakenly given De Vicenzo a 4 at the 17th rather than the 3. De Vicenzo had not noticed the mistake, signed and returned the score card, and rushed away from the scorer's table for press interviews. A little later, Aaron noticed the mistake and brought it to the attention of tournament officials.

Augusta National founder Bob Jones searched for a way around the ensuing ruling but none could be found. Once the score card was signed and returned, the decision under the Rules was straightforward: the higher score must stand. Goalby was the Masters Champion.

An hour later, De Vicenzo told the media, "It's my fault. Tommy feels like I feel, very bad. I think the Rule is hard." The day's drama was compounded by the fact that it was De Vincenzo's 45th birthday.

Failure to sign his first round score card arguably cost Padraig

Harrington the 2000 Benson and Hedges International Open at The Belfry. As he began warming up for the final round, holding a five-shot lead, the 28-year-old Irishman was informed by officials of a problem.

Members of the Committee had begun to collect Harrington's three previous score cards for souvenir purposes when it was noticed that he had not signed his first round card. Jamie Spence, his marker, had signed the card as required, but Michael Campbell, the other player in the group had mistakenly signed instead of Harrington. The resulting penalty under Rule 6-6b was disqualification.

RULE

PRACTICE

DEFINITIONS

All defined terms are in *italics* and are listed alphabetically in the Definitions section – see pages 6–15.

7-1. BEFORE OR BETWEEN ROUNDS
a. Match Play
On any day of a match play competition, a player may practise on the competition *course* before a round.

See **incident** involving Rule 7-1 on page 39

b. Stroke Play
Before a round or play-off on any day of a stroke play competition, a *competitor* must not practise on the competition *course* or test the surface of any *putting green* on the *course* by rolling a ball or roughening or scraping the surface.

When two or more rounds of a stroke play competition are to be played over consecutive days, a competitor must not practise between those rounds on any competition *course* remaining to be played, or test the surface of any *putting green* on such *course* by rolling a ball or roughening or scraping the surface.

Exception: Practice putting or chipping on or near the first *teeing ground* before starting a round or play-off is permitted.

PENALTY FOR BREACH OF RULE 7-1b:
Disqualification.

Note: The *Committee* may, in the conditions of a competition (Rule 33-1), prohibit practice on the competition *course* on any day of a match play competition or permit practise on the competition *course* or part of the *course* (Rule 33-2c) on any day of or between rounds of a stroke play competition.

See **incident** involving Rule 7-2 on page 39–40

7-2. DURING ROUND
A player must not make a practice stroke during play of a hole.

Between the play of two holes a player must not make a practice *stroke*, except that he may practice putting or chipping on or near:
(a) the *putting green* of the hole last played,
(b) any practice *putting green*, or
(c) the *teeing ground* of the next hole to be played in the round,

PRACTICE DURING A ROUND

Practice putting and chipping on or near the tee of the next hole to be played is permitted as long as play is not delayed.

provided a practice *stroke* is not made from a *hazard* and does not unduly delay play (Rule 6-7).

Strokes made in continuing the play of a hole, the result of which has been decided, are not practice *strokes*.

Exception: When play has been suspended by the *Committee*, a player may, prior to resumption of play, practise (a) as provided in this Rule, (b) anywhere other than on the competition *course* and (c) as otherwise permitted by the *Committee*.

PENALTY FOR BREACH OF RULE 7-2:

Match play – Loss of hole; Stroke play – Two strokes.

In the event of a breach between the play of two holes, the penalty applies to the next hole.

Note 1: A practice swing is not a practice *stroke* and may be taken at any place, provided the player does not breach the *Rules*.

Note 2: The *Committee* may, in the conditions of a competition (Rule 33-1), prohibit:

(a)   practice on or near the *putting green* of the hole last played, and

(b)   rolling a ball on the *putting green* of the hole last played.

RULE 7 INCIDENTS

The former Masters and Open Champion, Sandy Lyle, was disqualified from the 2000 Hope Chrysler Classic for practising between rounds during the Tournament.

After play had been completed in the third round, a member of the greenstaff was surprised to see Lyle practising on the 18th green and mentioned it to a member of the Tournament Committee. When officials asked Lyle about his actions and the player confirmed that he had returned to the 18th green to practise his putting, the Committee had no option but to disqualify him for a breach of Rule 7-1b.

After a suspension of play during the fourth round of the 2001

Players Championship at Sawgrass, both the penultimate group and the final group were required to resume play from the 10th tee. Tiger Woods, playing in the final group, was aware that the group in front would resume play first and that he would have additional time to arrive at the 10th tee.

Officials, concerned that Woods may have continued to hit practice shots on the practice range after the signal for a resumption of play had been sounded, advised Woods that such action would be in breach of Rule 7-2. Play was resumed without incident and Woods went on to win The Players Championship by one stroke from Vijay Singh.

RULE **8** ADVICE; INDICATING LINE OF PLAY

DEFINITIONS

All defined terms are in *italics* and are listed alphabetically in the Definitions section – see pages 6–15.

See **incident** involving Rule 8-1 on page 41–42

8-1. ADVICE
During a *stipulated round*, a player must not:
(a) give *advice* to anyone in the competition playing on the *course* other than his *partner*, or
(b) ask for *advice* from anyone other than his *partner* or either of their *caddies*.

8-2. INDICATING LINE OF PLAY
a. Other Than on Putting Green
Except on the *putting green*, a player may have the *line of play* indicated to him by anyone, but no one may be positioned by the player on or close to the line or an extension of the line beyond the *hole* while the *stroke* is being

ADVICE

made. Any mark placed by the player or with his knowledge to indicate the line must be removed before the *stroke* is made.

Exception: *Flagstick* attended or held up – see Rule 17-1.

b. On the Putting Green

See **incident** involving Rule 8-2b below

When the player's ball is on the *putting green*, the player, his *partner* or either of their *caddies* may, before but not during the *stroke*, point out a line for putting, but in so doing the *putting green* must not be touched. A mark must not be placed anywhere to indicate a line for putting.

PENALTY FOR BREACH OF RULE:
Match play – Loss of hole; Stroke play – Two strokes.

Note: The *Committee* may, in the conditions of a team competition (Rule 33-1), permit each team to appoint one person who may give *advice* (including pointing out a line for putting) to members of that team. The *Committee* may establish conditions relating to the appointment and permitted conduct of that person, who must be identified to the *Committee* before giving *advice*.

RULE 8 INCIDENTS

During the third round of the 1991 PGA Championship while advising John Daly about the break of a putt on Crooked Stick's 11th green, Daly's caddie, Jeff "Squeeky" Medlen, accidentally touched the green with the flagstick.

As ninth alternate, Daly had been included in the championship field when Nick Price withdrew to be present at the birth of his child, and three alternates ahead of Daly declined for various reasons. The unknown Arkansan had taken the outright lead for the title after posting a 69 and 67 for the first and second rounds respectively. Playing with Bruce Lietzke on Saturday, Daly was on his way to a third round

69. At the 11th, Medlen used his hand to point out the line of Daly's first putt. In his other hand, Medlen held the flagstick and inadvertently allowed it to touch the green.

The potential breach of the rules was televised to millions and, fortunately, videotaped for review. Alerted almost immediately to what had taken place, Rules officials met Daly at the end of the round to discuss the matter and make a decision before Daly returned his score card.

Daly, Medlen, Lietzke and Rules officials reviewed the videotape. The tape showed Medlen holding the removed flagstick and allowing it to touch the putting green about three feet to the right of the hole while indicating the line of putt with his other hand. Rule 8-2 states that, while a line for putting may be pointed out, the green shall not be touched in doing so.

After speaking with all involved and watching the tape, officials were satisfied that no penalty was incurred. Daly returned his third round card with a score of 69. The following day, he won the PGA Championship by three shots.

That part of Rule 8 relating to giving or asking for advice states, in part, that a player must not give advice to anyone in the competition except his partner. In the final round of the 1980 Tournament of Champions Tom Watson was playing with Lee Trevino. Having played together so often over the years, Watson knew Trevino's swing well and noticed a little flaw in it that day. He casually told Trevino about it. The television commentator at the time noted it as a friendly gesture between two tournament players, but viewers called in to point out that such assistance constituted giving advice, contrary to Rule 8-1.

After the round, Watson was asked whether he had given Trevino some guidance on his swing and a reply in the affirmative resulted in Watson incurring a two stroke penalty under the advice Rule. Fortunately, Watson had a three stroke lead at the conclusion of the 72 holes and the imposition of the two stroke penalty did not, therefore, prevent him from winning the Tournament.

RULE  INFORMATION AS TO STROKES TAKEN

DEFINITIONS

All defined terms are in *italics* and are listed alphabetically in the Definitions section – see pages 6–15.

9-1. GENERAL

The number of *strokes* a player has taken includes any *penalty strokes* incurred.

9-2. MATCH PLAY
a. Information as to Strokes Taken

An opponent is entitled to ascertain from the player, during the play of a hole, the number of *strokes* he has taken and, after play of a hole, the number of *strokes* taken on the hole just completed.

See **incident** involving Rule 9-2 on page 44–45

b. Wrong Information

A player must not give wrong information to his opponent. If a player gives wrong information, **he loses the hole.**

A player is deemed to have given wrong information if he:

(i)   fails to inform his opponent as soon as practicable that he has incurred a penalty, unless (a) he was obviously proceeding under a *Rule* involving a penalty and this was observed by his opponent, or (b) he corrects the mistake before his opponent makes his next stroke; or

(ii)   gives incorrect information during play of a hole regarding the number of *strokes* taken and does not correct the mistake before his opponent makes his next *stroke*; or

(iii)   gives incorrect information regarding the number of *strokes* taken to complete a hole and this affects the opponent's understanding of the result of the hole, unless he corrects the mistake before any player makes a *stroke* from the next *teeing ground* or, in the case of the last hole of the match, before all players leave the *putting green*.

A player has given wrong information even if it is due to the failure to include a penalty that he did not know he had incurred. It is the player's responsibility to know the *Rules*.

9-3. STROKE PLAY

A *competitor* who has incurred a penalty should inform his *marker* as soon as practicable.

Seve Ballesteros plays his tee shot from the 10th tee at Kiawah Island during the 1991 Ryder Cup, having called for a ruling for a possible breach of Rule 9-2.

RULE 9 INCIDENT

On the 7th tee of Kiawah Island's Ocean Course during the first mornings foursomes of the 1991 Ryder Cup Matches, Chip Beck and Paul Azinger were overheard by their European opponents discussing which type of ball they would use to optimise their performance during the play of that hole.

The Americans mistakenly believed that because one of them played a 90-compression ball and the other a 100-compression ball, they were entitled to a choice as to which they could use.

A variation of the "One-Ball Condition" was in effect which allowed both players to play their preferred brand and type of ball when it was their turn to play from the tee. However, once that determination was made on the first two holes, each player was limited to using that brand and type of ball thereafter.

Unknowingly and mistakenly, the Americans made the choice and the wrong type of ball was played from the tee. The European side of Seve Ballesteros and Jose Maria Olazabal suspected this was a breach of the Rules. Sam Torrance, a European team member who was not playing in the first morning's matches, was in the gallery and following the match. He was motioned over by Ballesteros, told of the situation and sent to fetch the European Captain Bernard Gallacher.

While Gallacher was being located, play of the 7th, 8th and 9th holes was completed. On the way to the 10th tee, the Europeans made a claim concerning what had taken place at the 7th hole. The chief referee was called to settle the dispute.

In match play, Rule 9-2 requires a player who has incurred a penalty to notify his opponent as soon as practicable. If he does not, even when he doesn't know he has incurred a penalty, he is considered to have given wrong information. In this case, the American side gave wrong information as a penalty was associated with their playing of the wrong type of ball from the 7th tee. However, since the European side was aware of the error and did not make a claim (Rule 2-5) before anyone played from the 8th tee, their belated claim could not be considered.

The match continued from the 10th tee without Beck and Azinger being penalised for their breach at the 7th hole.

RULE 10 — ORDER OF PLAY

DEFINITIONS

All defined terms are in *italics* and are listed alphabetically in the Definitions section – see pages 6–15.

10-1. MATCH PLAY
a. When Starting Play of Hole
The *side* that has the *honour* at the first *teeing ground* is determined by the order of the draw. In the absence of a draw, the *honour* should be decided by lot.

The *side* that wins a hole takes the *honour* at the next *teeing ground*. If a hole has been halved, the *side* that had the *honour* at the previous *teeing ground* retains it.

See **incident** involving Rule 10-1b on page 47

b. During Play of Hole
After both players have started play of the hole, the ball farther from the *hole* is played first. If the balls are equidistant from the *hole* or their positions relative to the *hole* are not determinable, the ball to be played first should be decided by lot.
Exception: Rule 30-3c (*best-ball* and *four-ball* match play).
Note: When the original ball is not to be played as it lies and the player is required to play a ball as nearly as possible at the spot from which the original ball was last played (see Rule 20-5), the order of play is determined by the spot from which the previous *stroke* was made. When a ball may be played from a spot other than where the previous *stroke* was made, the order of play is determined by the position where the original ball came to rest.

c. Playing Out of Turn
If a player plays when his opponent should have played, there is no penalty, but the opponent may immediately require the player to cancel the *stroke* so made and, in correct order, play a ball as nearly as possible at the spot from which the original ball was last played (see Rule 20-5).

10-2. STROKE PLAY
a. When Starting Play of Hole
The *competitor* who has the *honour* at the first *teeing ground* is determined by the order of the draw. In the absence of a draw, the *honour* should be decided by lot.

45

USA Captain, Pat Bradley, discusses with Pat Hurst and Kelly Robbins their options before requiring Annika Sorenstam, who had played out of turn, to replay her chip shot at the 13th hole during the 2000 Solheim Cup.

The *competitor* with the lowest score at a hole takes the *honour* at the next *teeing ground*. The *competitor* with the second lowest score plays next and so on. If two or more *competitors* have the same score at a hole, they play from the next *teeing ground* in the same order as at the previous *teeing ground*.

b. During Play of Hole

After the *competitors* have started play of the hole, the ball farthest from the *hole* is played first. If two or more balls are equidistant from the *hole* or their positions relative to the *hole* are not determinable, the ball to be played first should be decided by lot.

Exceptions: Rules 22 (ball assisting or interfering with play) and 31-5 (*four-ball* stroke play).

Note: When the original ball is not to be played as it lies and the player is required to play a ball as nearly as possible at the spot from which the original ball was last played (see Rule 20-5), the order of play is determined by the spot from which the previous *stroke* was made. When a ball may be played from a spot other than where the previous *stroke* was made, the order of play is determined by the position where the original ball came to rest.

c. Playing Out of Turn

If a *competitor* plays out of turn, there is no penalty and the ball is played as it lies. If, however, the *Committee* determines that *competitors* have agreed to play out of turn to give one of them an advantage, **they are disqualified**. (Making stroke while another ball in motion after stroke from putting green – see Rule 16-1f.)

(Incorrect order of play in threesomes and foursomes stroke play – see Rule 29-3.)

10-3. PROVISIONAL BALL OR SECOND BALL FROM TEEING GROUND

If a player plays a *provisional ball* or a second ball from a *teeing ground*, he must do so after his opponent or *fellow-competitor* has played his first *stroke*. If a player plays a *provisional ball* or a second ball out of turn, Rule 10-1c or -2c applies.

RULE 10 INCIDENT

After a suspension of play due to the course being in an unplayable condition during the 2000 Solheim Cup at Loch Lomond, Annika Sorenstam and Janice Moodie of the European Team returned to the 13th hole to resume their four-ball match against Kelly Robbins and Pat Hurst of the USA.

All four players were required to replace their balls in the spots from which they were lifted, as required by Rule 6-8d. Hurst was first to play from the fairway, with the other three balls either on or close to the putting green. Sorenstam played next, holing her chip from just off the green for a birdie 4.

Robbins, who had been talking to Hurst, walked back to where her ball marker lay to replace her ball on the putting green, then realised that it had been her turn to play and that Sorenstam had played out of turn. Rule 10-2b provides that the ball farther from the hole shall be played first and, in match play, if a player plays when her opponent should have played the opponent may require the player to cancel and replay the stroke in the correct order.

As Sorenstam had holed her chip shot it was clearly advantageous for the Americans to have the stroke cancelled and replayed. However, uncertain of whether to exercise their right they consulted with non-playing captain, Pat Bradley. After this consultation the Referee was advised that Sorenstam would be required to replay the stroke, which she failed to hole a second time. The hole was won by the Americans, with Pat Hurst making a birdie, and they went on to win the match by 2&1.

RULE 11 | TEEING GROUND

All defined terms are in *italics* and are listed alphabetically in the Definitions section – see pages 6–15.

11-1. TEEING

When the player's ball is to be teed within the *teeing ground*, it must be placed on:
- the surface of the *teeing ground*, including an irregularity of surface (whether or not created by the player), or
- a *tee* placed in or on the surface of the *teeing ground*, or
- sand or other natural substance placed on the surface of the *teeing ground*.

A player may stand outside the *teeing ground* to play a ball within it.

In teeing, if a player uses a non-conforming *tee* or any other object to raise the ball off the ground, **he is disqualified**.

11-2. TEE-MARKERS

Before a player makes his first *stroke* with any ball on the *teeing ground* of the hole being played, the tee-markers are deemed to be fixed. In these circumstances, if the player moves or allows to be moved a tee-marker for the purpose of avoiding interference with his *stance*, the area of his intended swing or his *line of play*, **he incurs the penalty for a breach of Rule 13-2**.

11-3. BALL FALLING OFF TEE

If a ball, when not *in play*, falls off a *tee* or is knocked off a *tee* by the player in *addressing* it, it may be re-teed without penalty. However, if a *stroke* is made at the ball in these circumstances, whether the ball is moving or not, the *stroke* counts but there is no penalty.

11-4. PLAYING FROM OUTSIDE TEEING GROUND
a. Match Play

If a player, when starting a hole, plays a ball from outside the *teeing ground* there is no penalty, but the opponent may immediately require the player to cancel the stroke and play a ball from within the *teeing ground*.

b. Stroke Play

See **incident** involving Rule 11-4b below

If a *competitor*, when starting a hole, plays a ball from outside the *teeing ground*, **he incurs a penalty of two strokes** and must then play a ball from within the *teeing ground*.

If the *competitor* plays a *stroke* from the next *teeing ground* without first correcting his mistake or, in the case of the last hole of the round, leaves the *putting green* without first declaring his intention to correct his mistake, **he is disqualified.**

The *stroke* from outside the *teeing ground* and any subsequent *strokes* by the *competitor* on the hole prior to his correction of the mistake do not count in his score.

11-5. PLAYING FROM WRONG TEEING GROUND

The provisions of Rule 11-4 apply.

RULE 11 INCIDENT

At the 1990 US Open Championship the drama and competitive tension at Medinah Country Club had been intense all week. Hale Irwin had summoned a wave of talent reflective of his 33 professional victories, which included two previous U.S. Open victories in 1974 and 1979. Indeed, he had holed a 45-foot birdie putt on the 72nd hole of play to force 18 hole play-off with Mike Donald whose only PGA Tour victory had come the previous year in Williamsburg, Virginia.

Mike Donald congratulates Hale Irwin after the 19th hole of the play-off for the 1990 US Open Championship – see incident above.

The players walked off the 17th green of the play-off round with Donald leading by one. On the 18th tee Mike Donald teed up in front of the markers. The walking Referee noticed whereupon Donald was asked to re-tee the ball.

Rule 11, as it applies to stroke play, is exact. If a competitor plays from outside the teeing ground, he shall incur a penalty of two strokes and shall then play a ball from within the teeing ground. Had Donald's mistake been observed a few moments later, after he had played from ahead of the markers, the resulting two-stroke penalty would have reversed that state of the play-off and given Irwin a one-stroke lead.

The Referee's intervention prevented the breach, but Donald's bogey at the 90th hole resulted in both men scoring 74 in the play-off round. By the terms and conditions outlined in the entry form, and for the first time in its history, the U.S. Open then moved to sudden death to determine the winner.

On the first sudden death hole, the 91st hole of the championship, Irwin holed a eight-foot birdie putt to become the U.S. Open's oldest winner.

RULE **12**

SEARCHING FOR AND IDENTIFYING BALL

DEFINITIONS

All defined terms are in *italics* and are listed alphabetically in the Definitions section – see pages 6–15.

See **incident** involving Rule 12-1 on page 52–53

12-1. SEARCHING FOR BALL; SEEING BALL

In searching for his ball anywhere on the *course*, the player may touch or bend long grass, rushes, bushes, whins, heather or the like, but only to the extent necessary to find and identify it, provided that this does not improve the lie of the ball, the area of his intended *stance* or swing or his *line of play*.

A player is not necessarily entitled to see his ball when making a *stroke*.

In a *hazard*, if a ball is believed to be covered by *loose impediments* or sand, the player may remove by probing or raking with a club or otherwise, as many *loose impediments* or as much sand as will enable him to see a part of the ball. If an excess is removed, there is no penalty and the ball must be re-covered so that only a part of it is visible. If the ball is *moved* during the removal, there is no penalty; the ball must be replaced and, if necessary, re-covered. As to removal of *loose impediments* outside a *hazard*, see Rule 23.

If a ball lying in an *abnormal ground condition* is accidentally *moved* during search, there is no penalty; the ball must be replaced, unless the player elects to proceed under Rule 25-1b. If the player replaces the ball, he may still proceed under Rule 25-1b if applicable.

If a ball is believed to be lying in water in a *water hazard*, the player may probe for it with a club or otherwise. If the ball is *moved* in probing, it must be replaced, unless the player elects to proceed under Rule 26-1. There is no penalty for causing the ball to *move* provided the movement of the ball was directly attributable to the specific act of probing. Otherwise, **the player incurs a penalty stroke under Rule 18-2a.**

SEARCHING FOR BALL IN BUNKER

If a player's ball is buried in a bunker, he may search for it by probing the sand with his fingers or he may use a rake. If the ball is moved, there is no penalty, but it must be replaced and, if necessary, re-covered so that only part of it is visible.

PENALTY FOR BREACH OF RULE 12-1:
Match play – loss of hole; Stroke play – Two strokes.

12-2. IDENTIFYING BALL

The responsibility for playing the proper ball rests with the player. Each player should put an identification mark on his ball.

Except in a hazard, if a player has reason to believe a ball is his, he may lift the ball without penalty to identify it.

Before lifting the ball, the player must announce his intention to his opponent in match play or his *marker* or a *fellow-competitor* in stroke play and mark the position of the ball. He may then lift the ball and identify it provided that he gives his opponent, *marker* or *fellow-competitor* an opportunity to observe the lifting and replacement. The ball must not be cleaned beyond the extent necessary for identification when lifted under Rule 12-2. If the player fails to comply with all or any part of this procedure, or he lifts his ball for identification in a *hazard*, **he incurs a penalty of one stroke.**

If the lifted ball is the player's ball he must replace it. If he fails to do so, **he**

51

incurs the general penalty for a breach of Rule 12-2, but there is no additional penalty under this Rule.

*PENALTY FOR BREACH OF RULE 12-2

Match play – Loss of hole; Stroke play – Two strokes.

*If a player incurs the general penalty for a breach of Rule 12-2, there is no additional penalty under this Rule.

RULE 12 INCIDENT

Nick Faldo discovered the Rule's protective nuances while searching for his ball in a tree at Pebble Beach's 14th hole during the 1992 U.S. Open.

His second shot at the 565-yard par 5 finished dangerously close to the out of bounds on the right of the hole. For his third shot, Faldo selected a short iron in order to play over the singular tree, which protects the elbow of the hole's second dogleg. As the ball climbed it struck the tree, but no one saw it fall back to earth.

Faldo asked the Rules official walking with the group if a provisional ball could be played. Because the official had not seen the ball come down, he replied that Faldo was entitled to play a provisional ball as the original might well be lost.

After playing the provisional ball and as they walked toward the

Golf balls can come to rest in some odd places. At the 1992 U.S. Open, Nick Faldo scaled a tree in search of his ball that had apparently come to rest there. See the story above.

tree to look for the original ball, Faldo asked the Rules official if it was permissible to climb the tree in order to search for his ball. The official advised that it was permissible, but cautioned him that if the ball moved while Faldo looked for it he would incur a penalty stroke and the ball would have to be replaced. Decision 18-2a/26 states exactly that.

However, the Rules official further advised Faldo that, if he stated his intention to declare his ball unplayable should he find it but before climbing or shaking the tree, there would be no penalty for moving the ball during the search. With such a prior notification, one penalty stroke would be assessed for a ball unplayable but no additional penalty would be incurred for moving the ball as provided in Decision 18-2a/27.

Faldo listened to the advice, declared that should he find his ball he intended to proceed under the unplayable ball Rule, and then climbed the tree to search for it. Having no luck, he shook the tree in hopes of dislodging the ball. It did not appear.

Unable to find his original ball, Faldo's provisional ball became the ball in play under penalty of stroke and distance.

RULE **13**

BALL PLAYED AS IT LIES

DEFINITIONS

All defined terms are in *italics* and are listed alphabetically in the Definitions section – see pages 6–15.

13-1. GENERAL
The ball must be played as it lies, except as otherwise provided in the *Rules*. (Ball at rest moved – see Rule 18)

See **incident** involving Rule 13-2 on page 56–57

13-2. IMPROVING LIE, AREA OF INTENDED STANCE OR SWING, OR LINE OF PLAY
A player must not improve or allow to be improved:
*   the position or lie of his ball,
*   the area of his intended *stance* or swing,
*   his *line of play* or a reasonable extension of that line beyond the *hole*, or
*   the area in which he is to drop or place a ball,
by any of the following actions:
*   moving, bending or breaking anything growing or fixed (including immovable *obstructions* and objects defining *out of bounds*),
*   creating or eliminating irregularities of surface,
*   removing or pressing down sand, loose soil, replaced divots or other cut turf placed in position, or
*   removing dew, frost or water.
However, the player incurs no penalty if the action occurs:
*   in fairly taking his *stance*,
*   in making a *stroke* or the backward movement of his club for a *stroke* and the *stroke* is made,
*   on the *teeing ground* in creating or eliminating irregularities of surface (Rule 11-1), or

53

IMPROVING AREA OF INTENDED SWING OR LINE OF PLAY

A player must not break an interfering branch or remove sand which is off the putting green but on the line of play.

- on the *putting green* in removing sand and loose soil or in repairing damage (Rule 16-1)

The club may be grounded only lightly and must not be pressed on the ground.

Exception: Ball in *hazard* – see Rule 13-4.

13-3. BUILDING STANCE

A player is entitled to place his feet firmly in taking his *stance*, but he must not build a *stance*.

See **incident** involving Rule 13-3 on page 56–57

13-4. BALL IN HAZARD; PROHIBITED ACTIONS

See **incident** involving Rule 13-4 on page 131–132

Except as provided in the *Rules*, before making a *stroke* at a ball that is in a *hazard* (whether a *bunker* or a *water hazard*) or that, having been lifted from a *hazard*, may be dropped or placed in the *hazard*, the player must not:

a. Test the condition of the *hazard* or any similar *hazard*;

b. Touch the ground in the *hazard* or water in the *water hazard* with his hand or a club; or

c. Touch or move a *loose impediment* lying in or touching the *hazard*.

Exceptions:

1. Provided nothing is done that constitutes testing the condition of the *hazard* or improves the lie of the ball, there is no penalty if the player (a) touches the ground in any *hazard* or water in a *water hazard* as a result of or to prevent falling, in removing an *obstruction*, in measuring or in retrieving, lifting, placing or replacing a ball under any *Rule* or (b) places his clubs in a *hazard*.

2. After making the *stroke*, the player or his *caddie* may smooth sand or soil in the *hazard*, provided that, if the ball is still in the *hazard* or has been lifted from the *hazard* and may be dropped or placed in the *hazard*, nothing is done that improves the lie of the ball or assists the player in his subsequent play of the hole.

Note: At any time, including at *address* or in the backward movement for the *stroke*, the player may touch with a club or otherwise any *obstruction*, any construction declared by the *Committee* to be an integral part of the *course* or any grass, bush, tree or other growing thing.

PENALTY FOR BREACH OF RULE:

Match play – Loss of hole; Stroke play – Two strokes.

(Searching for ball – see Rule 12-1)

(Relief for ball in water hazard – see Rule 26)

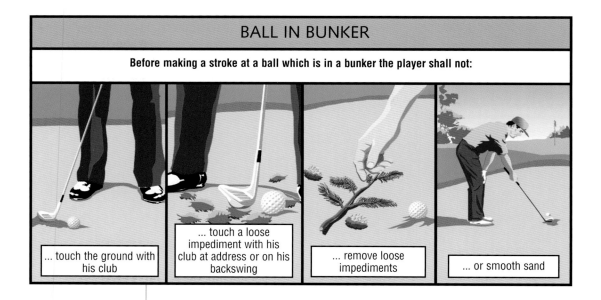

BALL IN BUNKER

Before making a stroke at a ball which is in a bunker the player shall not:

... touch the ground with his club

... touch a loose impediment with his club at address or on his backswing

... remove loose impediments

... or smooth sand

RULE 13 INCIDENTS

Bernhard Langer, playing the 9th hole at Wentworth in the 1999 Volvo PGA Championship was uncharacteristically careless when taking a practice swing near his ball which lay in rough near some trees. In so doing, he knocked down some leaves from a tree, an act which could have cost him a two stroke penalty. The Tournament Committee interviewed the player immediately after he had completed his round and reviewed the television replay several times, latterly with the player, in order to determine whether Langer should be penalised under Rule 13-2 for improving the area of his intended swing. However, after due consideration it was decided that Langer's knocking down of leaves had not resulted in any improvement in the area of intended swing when he came to play the stroke. Consequently, he was not penalised.

Craig Stadler returns to Torry Pines in 1995 and recreates the stroke for the assembled media.

In the third round of a US Tour event at Torry Pines near San Diego in 1987, when playing from underneath the branches of a tree, Craig Stadler unwittingly breached Rule 13-3 when he knelt on a towel to keep his trousers dry. Rule 13-3 states that a player is entitled to place his feet firmly in taking a stance but he must not build a stance. Prior to the incident, Decision 13-3/2 had been published stating that the act of kneeling on a towel, in such circumstances, was deemed to be building a stance.

A television viewer watching recorded coverage of the earlier rounds brought the incident to the attention of Tournament officials during the final round of the competition. Unfortunately, because Stadler had returned his score card for the third round containing a score for a hole lower than actually taken he was disqualified under Rule 6-6d.

However, in 1995 Stadler had the satisfaction of returning to Torry Pines to assist in cutting down the tree that was now dying of a fungus infection. He also recreated his stroke for the assembled media.

RULE **14** STRIKING THE BALL

DEFINITIONS All defined terms are in *italics* and are listed alphabetically in the Definitions section – see pages 6–15.

14-1. BALL TO BE FAIRLY STRUCK AT
The ball must be fairly struck at with the head of the club and must not be pushed, scraped or spooned.

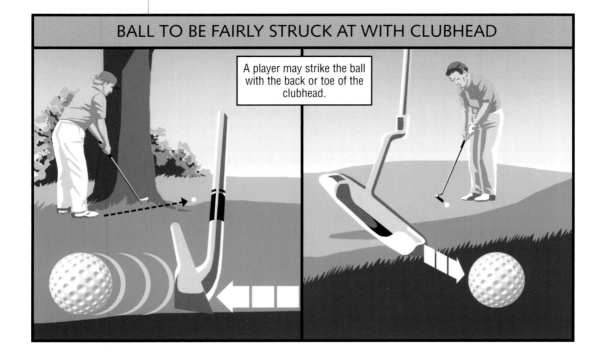

BALL TO BE FAIRLY STRUCK AT WITH CLUBHEAD

A player may strike the ball with the back or toe of the clubhead.

See **incident** involving Rule 14-2 on page 60

14-2. ASSISTANCE

In making a *stroke*, a player must not:

a. accept physical assistance or protection from the elements; or

b. allow his *caddie*, his *partner* or his *partner's caddie* to position himself on or close to an extension of the *line of play* or the *line of putt* behind the ball.

PENALTY FOR BREACH OF RULE 14-1 or -2:

Match play – Loss of hole; Stroke play – Two strokes.

14-3. ARTIFICIAL DEVICES AND UNUSUAL EQUIPMENT

The *R&A* reserves the right, at any time, to change the Rules relating to artificial devices and unusual equipment and make or change the

interpretations relating to these Rules.

A player in doubt as to whether use of an item would constitute a breach of Rule 14-3 should consult the *R&A*.

A manufacturer may submit to the *R&A* a sample of an item to be manufactured for a ruling as to whether its use during a *stipulated round* would cause a player to be in breach of Rule 14-3. The sample becomes the property of the *R&A* for reference purposes. If a manufacturer fails to submit a sample before manufacturing and/or marketing the item, the manufacturer assumes the risk of a ruling that use of the item would be contrary to the *Rules*.

Except as provided in the *Rules*, during a *stipulated round* the player must not use any artificial device or unusual equipment:

a. That might assist him in making a *stroke* or in his play; or

b. For the purpose of gauging or measuring distance or conditions that might affect his play; or

c. That might assist him in gripping the club, except that:

(i) plain gloves may be worn;

(ii) resin, powder and drying or moisturising agents may be used; and

(iii) a towel or handkerchief may be wrapped around the grip.

PENALTY FOR BREACH OF RULE 14-3:

Disqualification.

14-4. STRIKING THE BALL MORE THAN ONCE

If a player's club strikes the ball more than once in the course of a *stroke*, the player must count the *stroke* and **add a penalty stroke**, making two *strokes* in all.

See **incident** involving Rule 14-4 on page 60

14-5. PLAYING MOVING BALL

A player must not make a *stroke* at his ball while it is moving.

Exceptions:
* Ball falling off *tee* – Rule 11-3
* Striking the ball more than once – Rule 14-4
* Ball moving in water – Rule 14-6

When the ball begins to *move* only after the player has begun the *stroke* or the backward movement of his club for the *stroke*, he incurs no penalty under this Rule for playing a moving ball, but he is not exempt from any penalty under the following *Rules*:
* Ball at rest *moved* by player – Rule 18-2a
* Ball at rest moving after *address* – Rule 18-2b

(Ball purposely deflected or stopped by player, partner or caddie – see Rule 1-2)

14-6. BALL MOVING IN WATER

When a ball is moving in water in a *water hazard*, the player may, without penalty, make a *stroke*, but he must not delay making his *stroke* in order to allow the wind or current to improve the position of the ball. A ball moving in water in a *water hazard* may be lifted if the player elects to invoke Rule 26.

PENALTY FOR BREACH OF RULE 14-5 or 14-6:

Match play – Loss of hole; Stroke play – Two strokes.

RULE 14 INCIDENTS

On a rainy day at the 1995 British Masters at Collingtree Park, Domingo Hospital's first putt on the 11th hole, came to rest just a few inches from the hole. His caddie walked with him holding an umbrella over Hospital's head. Unfortunately, as Hospital putted out his caddie still had the umbrella over his head and, therefore, the player incurred a penalty of two strokes under Rule 14-2a for accepting protection from the elements.

If Hospital had held the umbrella himself he would not have incurred any penalty as a player may protect himself from the elements. However, he must not accept such protection from anyone else.

With 14 holes to play in the 1985 US Open T. C. Chen led the Championship by four strokes when his ball finished in thick rough to the right of the 5th green at Oakland Hills.

In attempting to play a delicate chip his club struck the ball twice during the stroke. In such a situation Rule 14-4 provides that the player shall count the stroke and add a penalty stroke, making two strokes in all. The second strike of the ball pushed it a little higher in the air and slightly to Chen's left. It came to rest on the apron of the putting green about ten feet from the hole. Visibly shaken, Chen took three more to finish the hole for an eight and his four stroke lead had evaporated on one hole. Indeed, he ultimately tied for second with Denis Watson and Dave Barr, just one shot behind Andy North.

One of golf's most infamous Rules situations involved T.C. Chen at the 1985 U.S. Open. This incident, which had a dramatic effect on the final results of the championship, is retold on this page.

RULE 15 SUBSTITUTED BALL; WRONG BALL

DEFINITIONS

All defined terms are in *italics* and are listed alphabetically in the Definitions section – see pages 6–15.

15-1. GENERAL

A player must hole out with the ball played from the *teeing ground* unless the ball is *lost, out of bounds* or the player *substitutes* another ball, whether or not substitution is permitted (see Rule 15-2). If a player plays a *wrong ball*, see Rule 15-3.

15-2. SUBSTITUTED BALL

A player may *substitute* a ball when proceeding under a *Rule* that permits the player to play, drop or place another ball in completing the play of a hole. The *substituted ball* becomes the *ball in play*.

   If a player *substitutes* a ball when not permitted to do so under the *Rules*, that *substituted ball* is not a *wrong ball*; it becomes the *ball in play*. If the mistake is not corrected as provided in Rule 20-6 and the player makes a *stroke* at a wrongly *substituted ball*, **he incurs the penalty prescribed by the applicable Rule** and, in stroke play, must play out the hole with the *substituted ball*.
(Playing from Wrong Place – see Rule 20-7)

15-3. WRONG BALL
a. Match Play

If a player makes a *stroke* at a *wrong ball* that is not in a *hazard*, **he loses the hole**.

PLAYING A SUBSTITUTED BALL

I lifted my ball from the putting green to clean it, but I have just noticed that I have played the other ball I had in my pocket.

Unfortunately, you have substituted a ball when not permitted to do so. It is now the ball in play and you incur a two-stroke penalty. If we had been playing a match you would have lost the hole.

There is no penalty if a player makes a *stroke* at a *wrong ball* in a *hazard*. Any *strokes* made at a *wrong ball* in a *hazard* do not count in the player's score.

If the *wrong ball* belongs to another player, its owner must place a ball on the spot from which the *wrong ball* was first played.

If the player and opponent exchange balls during the play of a hole, the first to make a *stroke* at the *wrong ball* that is not in a *hazard*, **loses the hole;** when this cannot be determined, the hole must be played out with the balls exchanged.

b. Stroke Play

See **incident** involving Rule 15-3 below

If a *competitor* makes a *stroke* or *strokes* at a *wrong ball* that is not in a *hazard*, **he incurs a penalty of two strokes**.

There is no penalty if a *competitor* makes a *stroke* at a *wrong ball* in a *hazard*. Any *strokes* made at a *wrong ball* in a *hazard* do not count in the *competitor's* score.

The *competitor* must correct his mistake by playing the correct ball or by proceeding under the *Rules*. If he fails to correct his mistake before making a *stroke* on the next *teeing ground* or, in the case of the last hole of the round, fails to declare his intention to correct his mistake before leaving the *putting green*, **he is disqualified**.

Strokes made by a *competitor* with a *wrong ball* do not count in his score.

If the *wrong ball* belongs to another *competitor*, its owner must place a ball on the spot from which the *wrong ball* was first played.

(Lie of ball to be placed or replaced altered – see Rule 20-3b)

(Spot not determinable – see Rule 20-3c)

RULE 15 INCIDENT

Nick Faldo turned a bad day into a disaster during the first round of the 1994 Open Championship at Turnberry. Two over par coming to the 17th hole, the weather deteriorated as Faldo was about to play from the tee. The driving rain and strong winds may go some way to explaining Faldo's errant shot and the fact that he did not see where his ball finished. Both Faldo and his fellow-competitor Jim McGovern pushed their drives into the right rough but Faldo's drive was shorter and wider than McGovern's. Faldo found a ball short of where McGovern was looking for his and played it.

However, Faldo had not checked that the ball was his before playing it, which seemed totally out of character for a player so meticulous in his approach to the game. Just a glimpse at the ball would have shown that it was not his but McGovern's as McGovern was playing a different brand.

Subsequent to Faldo playing his stroke, McGovern was advised that the other ball was in deep rough, something which confused him until he reached it, and saw that it belonged to Faldo. The mistake cost Faldo a two-stroke penalty under Rule 15-3 and, as required by this Rule, he had to correct his error by playing his own ball. Faldo completed the hole with a three over par 8, and his round in 75.

Faldo's mood certainly improved by the end of the week, a second round 66 meant that he made the cut and this score was improved on the final day with a 64 giving him a four round total of 275, 5 under par and a share of 8th place.

RULE **16**

THE PUTTING GREEN

DEFINITIONS

All defined terms are in *italics* and are listed alphabetically in the Definitions section – see pages 6–15.

16-1. GENERAL
a. Touching *Line of Putt*
The *line of putt* must not be touched except:
(i)   the player may remove *loose impediments*, provided he does not press anything down;
(ii) the player may place the club in front of the ball when *addressing* it, provided he does not press anything down;
(iii) in measuring – Rule 18-6;
(iv) in lifting the ball – Rule 16-1b;
(v)   in pressing down a ball-marker;
(vi) in repairing old *hole* plugs or ball marks on the *putting green* – Rule 16-1c; and
(vii) in removing movable *obstructions* – Rule 24-1
(Indicating line for putting on putting green – see Rule 8-2b)

b. Lifting and Cleaning Ball
A ball on the *putting green* may be lifted and, if desired, cleaned. The position of the ball must be marked before it is lifted and the ball must be replaced (see Rule 20-1).

c. Repair of Hole Plugs, Ball Marks and Other Damage
The player may repair an old *hole* plug or damage to the *putting green* caused

63

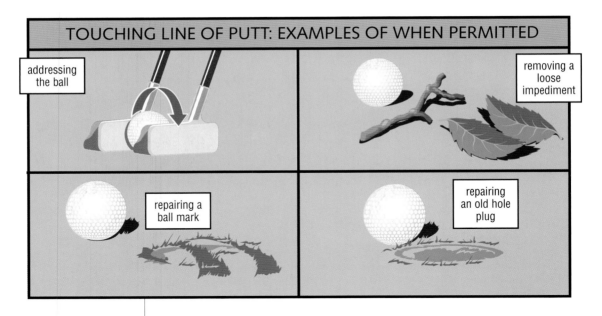

by the impact of a ball, whether or not the player's ball lies on the *putting green*. If a ball or ball-marker is accidentally *moved* in the process of the repair, the ball or ball-marker must be replaced. There is no penalty provided the movement of the ball is directly attributable to the specific act of repairing an old *hole* plug or damage to the *putting green* caused by the impact of a ball. Otherwise, **the player incurs a *penalty stroke* under Rule 18-2a.**

Any other damage to the *putting green* must not be repaired if it might assist the player in his subsequent play of the hole.

d. Testing Surface

During the play of a hole, a player must not test the surface of the *putting green* by rolling a ball or roughening or scraping the surface.

e. Standing Astride or on Line of Putt

The player must not make a *stroke* on the *putting green* from a *stance* astride, or with either foot touching, the *line of putt* or an extension of that line behind the ball.

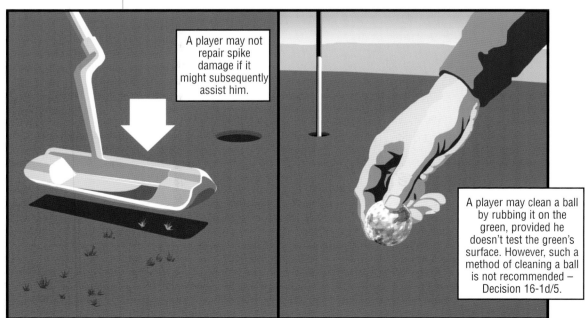

f. Making Stroke While Another Ball in Motion

The player must not make a *stroke* while another ball is in motion after a *stroke* from the *putting green*, except that, if a player does so, there is no penalty if it was his turn to play.

(Lifting ball assisting or interfering with play while another ball in motion – see Rule 22)

PENALTY FOR BREACH OF RULE 16-1:
Match play – Loss of hole; Stroke play – Two strokes.

(Position of caddie or partner – see Rule 14-2)

(Wrong putting green – see Rule 25-3)

16-2. BALL OVERHANGING HOLE

See **incidents** involving Rule 16-2 on page 67

When any part of the ball overhangs the lip of the *hole*, the player is allowed enough time to reach the *hole* without unreasonable delay and an additional ten seconds to determine whether the ball is at rest. If by then the ball has not fallen into the *hole*, it is deemed to be at rest. If the ball subsequently falls into the *hole*, the player is deemed to have *holed* out with his last *stroke*, and **must add a *penalty stroke* to his score** for the hole; otherwise, there is no penalty under this Rule.

(Undue delay – see Rule 6-7)

RULE 16 INCIDENTS

The Rule dealing with a ball overhanging the hole was revised as a result of an incident involving Denis Watson during play of the 8th hole in the first round of the 1985 U.S. Open at Oakland Hills Country Club.

From 10 feet, Watson putted and his ball stopped on the lip of the hole. After waiting an extended period of time, the ball fell in. Subsequently, Watson was told to add two penalty strokes to his score for undue delay as described at the time in Rule 16-1h.

The severe ramification of the penalty would not be clear for three more days when Watson would finish just one stroke behind the champion, Andy North.

In 1988, the Rule was moved to Rule 16-2 and a one-stroke penalty assigned to any breach.

The 2000 Qatar Masters highlighted the principles of Rule 16-2 in an intriguing incident involving Soren Hansen and Matthais Gronberg. Hansen's ten foot putt hovered over the edge of the hole before finally falling into the hole. Gronberg, one of Hansen's fellow-competitors announced he had been counting and since he got to 11 and the time limit was 10 seconds, he should add a penalty stroke to his score. Voices were raised above the wind and a Rules official was summoned.

After the official had listened to accounts of the incident from all witnesses he ruled that Hansen had incurred a penalty of one stroke under Rule 16-2. However, on returning to the Tournament office, the referee asked whether there was any television coverage of the incident available. Fortunately there was and this showed that, after Hansen being given a reasonable time to reach the hole, only eight seconds had elapsed when the ball fell into the hole and, consequently, the penalty was rescinded.

RULE **17** THE FLAGSTICK

DEFINITIONS

All defined terms are in *italics* and are listed alphabetically in the Definitions section – see pages 6–15.

17-1. FLAGSTICK ATTENDED, REMOVED OR HELD UP

Before making a *stroke* from anywhere on the *course*, the player may have the *flagstick* attended, removed or held up to indicate the position of the *hole*.

If the *flagstick* is not attended, removed or held up before the player makes a *stroke*, it must not be attended, removed or held up during the *stroke* or while the player's ball is in motion if doing so might influence the movement of the ball.

Note 1: If the *flagstick* is in the *hole* and anyone stands near it while a *stroke* is being made, he is deemed to be attending the *flagstick*.

Note 2: If, prior to the *stroke*, the *flagstick* is attended, removed or held up

67

by anyone with the player's knowledge and he makes no objection, the player is deemed to have authorised it.

Note 3: If anyone attends or holds up the *flagstick* while a *stroke* is being made, he is deemed to be attending the *flagstick* until the ball comes to rest.

17-2. UNAUTHORISED ATTENDANCE

If an opponent or his *caddie* in match play or a *fellow-competitor* or his *caddie* in stroke play, without the player's authority or prior knowledge, attends, removes or holds up the *flagstick* during the *stroke* or while the ball is in motion, and the act might influence the movement of the ball, the opponent or *fellow-competitor* incurs the applicable penalty.

*PENALTY FOR BREACH OF RULE 17-1 or 17-2

Match play – Loss of hole; Stroke play – Two strokes.

*In stroke play, if a breach of Rule 17-2 occurs and the *competitor's* ball subsequently strikes the *flagstick*, the person attending or holding it or anything carried by him, the *competitor* incurs no penalty. The ball is played as it lies except that, if the *stroke* was made on the *putting green*, the *stroke* is cancelled and the ball must be replaced and replayed.

17-3. BALL STRIKING FLAGSTICK OR ATTENDANT

See **incidents** involving Rule 17-3 on page 70–71

The player's ball must not strike:

a. The *flagstick* when it is being attended, removed or held up;

b. The person attending or holding up the *flagstick*; or

c. The *flagstick* in the *hole*, unattended, when the *stroke* has been made on the *putting green*.

Exception: When the *flagstick* is attended, removed or held up without the player's authority – see Rule 17-2.

PENALTY FOR BREACH OF RULE 17-3:

Match play – Loss of hole; Stroke play – Two strokes and the ball must be played as it lies.

BALL STRIKES FLAGSTICK LYING ON GREEN IN MATCH PLAY

17-4. BALL RESTING AGAINST FLAGSTICK

When the *flagstick* is in the *hole* and a player's ball when not *holed* rests against it, the player or another person authorised by him may move or remove the *flagstick* and if the ball falls into the *hole*, the player is deemed to have *holed* out with his last *stroke*; otherwise, the ball, if *moved*, must be placed on the lip of the *hole*, without penalty.

RULE 17 INCIDENTS

During the 1995 Open at St Andrews, Peter Fowler of Australia, found himself on the front edge of the second green of the Old Course, with the hole in the back left corner beyond the huge humps and swales that are a feature of the green. He asked the referee if he could play the stroke with a wedge. The Rules do not stipulate that a player must use a putter when his ball is on the green and, therefore, he was given the go-ahead and pitched to within three feet of the hole.

Corey Pavin was on the other half of this double green, playing the 16th. He congratulated Fowler on a great shot, but warned; "Next time have the flag attended. It's a two-shot penalty if you hit the stick." The fact that the ball was on the green and, therefore, Rule 17-3c could have been breached, had escaped everyone else's attention.

The incident repeated itself in the 2000 Open at the same hole, this time with Jack Nicklaus. Nicklaus had hit his second shot well to the left, on the 16th hole portion of the green, with a bunker between himself and the hole on the second. He floated up a perfect wedge shot that almost went in the hole. The referee accompanying the group was unsighted by the bunker and assumed that Nicklaus had played his shot from the fairway beyond the green.

As they walked to the next tee Nicklaus admitted that he was unsure if his ball was on the green or not and the referee reminded him that if he had played from the green he should have had the flag attended.

"I had a 40 yard pitch shot over a bunker," said Nicklaus after the round "You don't think much about having the pin attended. I've never done that before. It never entered my mind."

Miguel Angel Jimenez found himself in an awkward situation on Pebble Beach's 17th green during the 2000 U.S. Open. When the course was altered in 1929 the 17th green was redesigned into a large hour-glass shape divided by a diagonal ridge. The ridge running through its centre makes it play like a double green. Hence, when the hole is cut at back left, it is difficult for a ball played from front right to get close to the hole. This was Jimenez's dilemma.

The pinched, hourglass shape brought the rough into the line of putt necessary for him to get close to the hole. For this reason, he chose to play a pitch shot from over the rough and over the ridge to the hole on the other side of the green.

Jimenez was aware of the Rules regarding the flagstick, but he wisely sought confirmation from the referee walking with his group. Rule 17-3 states that a player's ball shall not strike the flagstick in the hole, unattended, when the ball has been played from the green. In order to avoid such a breach of the Rules, Jimenez directed his caddie to attend the flagstick.

Therefore, Jimenez's caddie would be required to remove the flagstick if it looked as though the ball might go in the hole.

Playing a delicate pitch, Jimenez took a small divot. His ball landed on the down slope of the ridge and ran to about 10 feet from the hole. From there he took two putts for bogey.

RULE **18** BALL AT REST MOVED

DEFINITIONS

All defined terms are in *italics* and are listed alphabetically in the Definitions section – see pages 6–15.

See **incident** involving Rule 18-1 on page 115–116

18-1. BY OUTSIDE AGENCY

If a ball at rest is *moved* by an *outside agency*, there is no penalty and the ball must be replaced.

(Player's ball at rest moved by another ball – see Rule 18-5)

See **incidents** involving Rule 18-2a on page 74

18-2. BY PLAYER, PARTNER, CADDIE OR EQUIPMENT
a. General

When a player's ball is *in play*, if:

(i)   the player, his *partner* or either of their *caddies* lifts or *moves* it, touches it purposely (except with a club in the act of *addressing* it) or causes it to *move* except as permitted by a *Rule*, or

(ii)   *equipment* of the player or his *partner* causes the ball to *move*,

the player incurs a penalty of one stroke. If the ball is *moved*, it must be replaced unless the movement of the ball occurs after the player has begun the *stroke* or the backward movement of the club for the *stroke* and the *stroke* is made.

Under the *Rules* there is no penalty if a player accidentally causes his ball to *move* in the following circumstances:

•   In searching for a ball in a *hazard* covered by *loose impediments* or sand, for a ball in an *abnormal ground condition* or for a ball believed to be in water in a *water hazard* – Rule 12-1

•   In repairing a *hole* plug or ball mark – Rule 16-1c

•   In measuring – Rule 18-6

•   In lifting a ball under a *Rule* – Rule 20-1

•   In placing or replacing a ball under a *Rule* – Rule 20-3a

•   In removing a *loose impediment* on the *putting green* – Rule 23-1

•   In removing movable *obstructions* – Rule 24-1

See **incident** involving Rule 18-2b on page 74

b. Ball Moving After Address

If a player's *ball in play moves* after he has *addressed* it (other than as a result of a *stroke*), the player is deemed to have *moved* the ball and **incurs a**

71

BALL AT REST MOVED

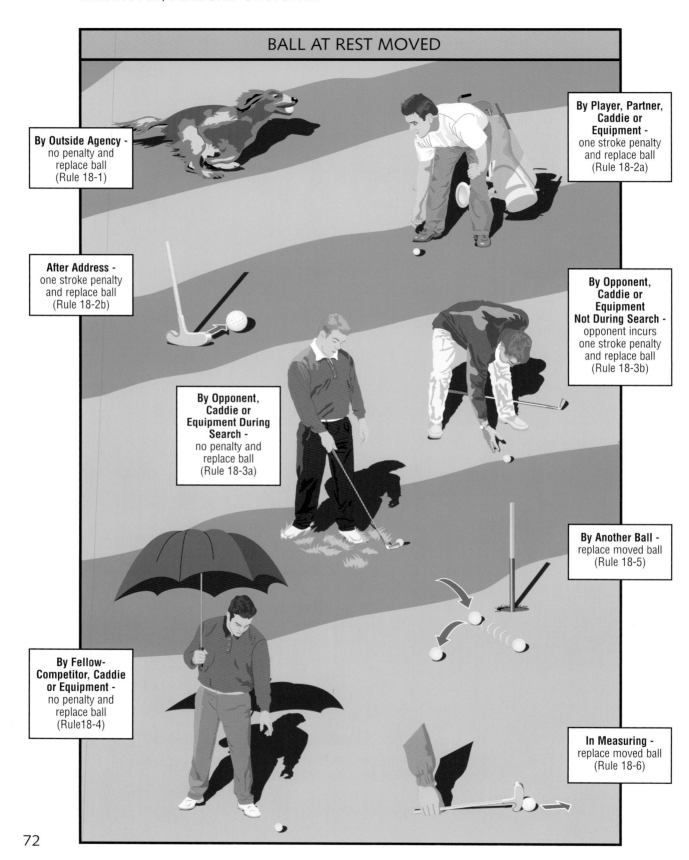

By Outside Agency -
no penalty and
replace ball
(Rule 18-1)

**By Player, Partner,
Caddie or
Equipment -**
one stroke penalty
and replace ball
(Rule 18-2a)

After Address -
one stroke penalty
and replace ball
(Rule 18-2b)

**By Opponent,
Caddie or
Equipment
Not During Search -**
opponent incurs
one stroke penalty
and replace ball
(Rule 18-3b)

**By Opponent,
Caddie or
Equipment During
Search -**
no penalty and
replace ball
(Rule 18-3a)

By Another Ball -
replace moved ball
(Rule 18-5)

**By Fellow-
Competitor, Caddie
or Equipment -**
no penalty and
replace ball
(Rule18-4)

In Measuring -
replace moved ball
(Rule 18-6)

penalty of one stroke. The ball must be replaced unless the movement of the ball occurs after the player has begun the *stroke* or the backward movement of the club for the *stroke* and the *stroke* is made.

18-3. BY OPPONENT, CADDIE OR EQUIPMENT IN MATCH PLAY
a. During Search
If, during search for a player's ball, an opponent, his *caddie* or his *equipment* *moves* the ball, touches it or causes it to *move*, there is no penalty. If the ball is *moved*, it must be replaced.

b. Other Than During Search
If, other than during search for a player's ball, an opponent, his *caddie* or his *equipment* *moves* the ball, touches it purposely or causes it to move, except as otherwise provided in the *Rules*, **the opponent incurs a penalty of one stroke**. If the ball is *moved*, it must be replaced.
(Playing a wrong ball - see Rule 15-3)
(Ball moved in measuring to determine which ball is farther from the hole - see Rule 18-6)

18-4. BY FELLOW-COMPETITOR, CADDIE OR EQUIPMENT IN STROKE PLAY
If a *fellow-competitor*, his *caddie* or his *equipment* *moves* the player's ball, touches it or causes it to *move*, there is no penalty. If the ball is *moved*, it must be replaced.
(Playing a wrong ball - see Rule 15-3).

18-5. BY ANOTHER BALL
If a *ball in play* and at rest is *moved* by another ball in motion after a stroke, the *moved* ball must be replaced.

18-6. BALL MOVED IN MEASURING
If a ball or ball-marker is *moved* in measuring while proceeding under or in determining the application of a *Rule*, the ball or ball-marker must be replaced. There is no penalty provided the movement of the ball or ball-marker is directly attributable to the specific act of measuring. Otherwise, **the provisions of Rules 18-2a, 18-3b or 18-4 apply.**

*PENALTY FOR BREACH OF RULE:
Match play - Loss of hole; Stroke play - Two strokes.
*If a player who is required to replace a ball fails to do so, he incurs the general penalty for breach of Rule 18. There is no additional penalty under Rule 18, except in the case of a wrongly *substituted* ball (Rule 15-2).

Note 1: If a ball to be replaced under this Rule is not immediately recoverable, another ball may be *substituted*.
Note 2: If the original lie of a ball to be placed or replaced has been altered, see Rule 20-3b.
Note 3: If it is impossible to determine the spot on which a ball is to be placed, see Rule 20-3c.

RULE 18 INCIDENTS

At the 1925 U.S. Open Championship at Worcester Country Club in Massachusetts, Bobby Jones saw his ball move after he addressed it on a steep bank at the 11th hole during the first round. Jones insisted that a penalty be added to his score. Often the player may be the only one who sees such a breach and, in such circumstances, must call the penalty on himself.

When praised for his honesty, Jones replied, "You just might as well praise me for not breaking into banks. There is only one way to play this game."

Jones began the final round in a tie for fourth place but was able to tie Willie Macfarlane to force a 36-hole play-off, which he lost by one stroke.

While executing his pre-shot routine before putting at the 17th hole in the 1997 Players Championship, David Love III's putter accidentally moved his ball about a foot. Failing to replace the moved ball, he two putted and went to the 18th tee. Assessing himself one stroke for moving his ball rather than the total penalty of two strokes for moving and not replacing his ball, Love recorded a four on his score card instead of a five.

Although viewed by thousands in person, the error was not brought to Love's attention until after his score card had been returned. The result was disqualification under Rule 6-6d for returning a score for a hole lower than actually taken.

On a particularly windy day at Royal Birkdale during the 1998 Open Championship, Per-Ulrik Johannson had played a good shot to the 8th green and was preparing to putt when a gust of wind caused his ball to move.

Immediately turning to the referee for assistance, he explained that the ball moved after he had placed his club behind the ball but before he had placed his feet in position for putting. The referee had to ascertain whether Johannson had completed his address procedure because, even though the wind had moved the ball, if the player had addressed it prior to this occurring he would be deemed to have moved it under Rule 18-2b, resulting in a one stroke penalty. Fortunately for Johannson, it was determined that at the time the ball moved he had not completed taking his stance and, therefore, in accordance with the Definition he had not addressed the ball. Therefore, he incurred no penalty and was required to play the ball from its new position.

RULE **19** BALL IN MOTION DEFLECTED OR STOPPED

DEFINITIONS

All defined terms are in *italics* and are listed alphabetically in the Definitions section – see pages 6–15.

19-1. BY OUTSIDE AGENCY

See **incident** involving Rule 19-1 on page 77–78

If a ball in motion is accidentally deflected or stopped by any *outside agency*, it is a *rub of the green*, there is no penalty and the ball must be played as it lies except:

a. If a ball in motion after a *stroke* other than on the *putting green* comes to rest in or on any moving or animate *outside agency*, the player must, *through the green* or in a *hazard*, drop the ball, or on the *putting green* place the ball, as near as possible to the spot where the *outside agency* was when the ball came to rest in or on it, and

b. If a ball in motion after a *stroke* on the *putting green* is deflected or stopped by, or comes to rest in or on, any moving or animate *outside agency* except a worm or an insect, the *stroke* is cancelled. The ball must be replaced and the *stroke* replayed.

   If the ball is not immediately recoverable, another ball may be *substituted*. (Player's ball deflected or stopped by another ball – see Rule 19-5)

Note: If the *referee* or the *Committee* determines that a player's ball has been purposely deflected or stopped by an *outside agency*, Rule 1-4 applies to the player. If the *outside agency* is a *fellow-competitor* or his *caddie*, Rule 1-2 applies to the *fellow-competitor*.

19-2. BY PLAYER, PARTNER, CADDIE OR EQUIPMENT
a. Match Play

See **incident** involving Rule 19-2 on page 77–78

If a player's ball is accidentally deflected or stopped by himself, his *partner* or either of their *caddies* or *equipment*, **he loses the hole**.

b. Stroke Play
If a *competitor's* ball is accidentally deflected or stopped by himself, his *partner* or either of their *caddies* or *equipment*, **the *competitor* incurs a penalty of two strokes**. The ball must be played as it lies, except when it comes to rest in or on the *competitor's*, his *partner's* or either of their *caddies'* clothes or *equipment*, in which case the *competitor* must *through the green* or in a *hazard* drop the ball, or on the *putting green* place the ball, as near as possible to where the article was when the ball came to rest in or on it.
Exception: Dropped ball – see Rule 20-2a.
(Ball purposely deflected or stopped by player, partner or caddie – see Rule 1-2)

19-3. BY OPPONENT, CADDIE OR EQUIPMENT IN MATCH PLAY
If a player's ball is accidentally deflected or stopped by an opponent, his *caddie* or his *equipment*, there is no penalty. The player may, before another *stroke* is made by either side, cancel the *stroke* and play a ball without penalty as nearly as possible at the spot from which the original ball was last played (see Rule 20-5) or he may play the ball as it lies. However, if the player elects not to cancel the *stroke* and the ball has come to rest in or on the opponent's or his *caddie's* clothes or *equipment*, the player must *through the green* or in a *hazard* drop the ball, or on the *putting green* place the ball, as near as possible to where the article was when the ball came to rest in or on it.
Exception: Ball striking person attending *flagstick* – see Rule 17-3b.
(Ball purposely deflected or stopped by opponent or caddie – see Rule 1-2)

19-4. BY FELLOW-COMPETITOR, CADDIE OR EQUIPMENT IN STROKE PLAY
See Rule 19-1 regarding ball deflected by *outside agency*.

BALL IN MOTION DEFLECTED OR STOPPED

By Player, Partner, Caddie or Equipment Match Play - player loses hole (Rule 19-2a)

By Player, Partner, Caddie or Equipment Stroke Play - player incurs penalty of two strokes and ball played as it lies (Rule 19-2b)

By Outside Agency - no penalty and ball played as it lies (Rule 19-1)

By Opponent, Caddie or Equipment Match Play - no penalty and ball played as it lies or stroke cancelled and replayed (Rule 19-3)

By Fellow-Competitor, Caddie or Equipment Stroke Play - see Rule 19-1 regarding ball deflected by Outside Agency (Rule 19-4)

By Another Ball at Rest - no penalty and ball played as it lies. Except in stroke play, if both balls lay on green prior to stroke, player incurs two stroke penalty (Rule 19-5a)

By Another Ball in Motion - no penalty and ball played as it lies, unless player in breach of Rule 16-1f (Rule 19-5b)

19-5. BY ANOTHER BALL
a. At Rest
If a player's ball in motion after a *stroke* is deflected or stopped by a *ball in play* and at rest, the player must play his ball as it lies. In match play, there is no penalty. In stroke play, there is no penalty unless both balls lay on the *putting green* prior to the *stroke*, in which case **the player incurs a penalty of two strokes**.

b. In Motion
If a player's ball in motion after a *stroke* is deflected or stopped by another ball in motion after a *stroke*, the player must play his ball as it lies. There is no penalty unless the player was in breach of Rule 16-1f, in which case **he incurs the penalty for breach of that Rule**.

Exception: If the player's ball is in motion after a *stroke* on the *putting green* and the other ball in motion is an *outside agency* – see Rule 19-1b.

PENALTY FOR BREACH OF RULE:
Match play – Loss of hole; Stroke play – Two strokes.

RULE 19 INCIDENTS

In the last round of the 1990 Australian Open Brett Ogle was just two shots off the lead playing the 17th hole. In an attempt to close the deficit he risked a difficult second shot around a tree with a 2 iron. Unfortunately, his ball struck the tree situated immediately in front of him and rebounded backwards, striking Ogle on the knee.

Apart from being extremely painful, Ogle suffered the indignity of a two stroke penalty under Rule 19-2 because the ball had struck him. Decision 6-8a/3 states that it is reasonable to allow a player ten or fifteen minutes to recuperate from such a physical problem. After being allowed time to recover, Ogle limped down the closing two holes, using his driver as a walking stick, followed by a team of helpers carrying bandages and ice packs behind him. He finished the 17th hole in 9 strokes, the ricochet costing him any chance of winning the title.

Ogle was in considerable pain on the Sunday night and an X-ray revealed a stellate fracture of the patella bone just below the knee.

Sergio Garcia encountered an unusual situation when his drive at Pebble Beach's 4th hole struck and killed a seagull during the second round of the 2000 U.S. Open.

The bird swooped down into the ball's path just 20 yards from the teeing ground. Travelling with great velocity, the ball struck the bird in the chest. The gull was killed. Somehow, the ball continued on in a decelerated way until it struck the top of the out of bounds fence, which shelters the beach club car park to the right of the hole. One bounce atop the picket fence and the ball was deflected back onto the course, where it settled in the rough.

Garcia was distraught by the bird's death and the bizarre rub of the green. In such a situation, no penalty is incurred and the ball must be played as it lies. At first, many of the assembled spectators thought such a ruling was unfair and Garcia should be allowed to replay the shot. Their concern was assuaged when it was pointed out that had Garcia's ball been deflected into the hole it would have been a hole-in-one.

In the final round of the 1990 Australian Open Brett Ogle incurred an injury and a two stroke penalty for a breach of Rule 19-2.

RULE **20**

LIFTING, DROPPING AND PLACING; PLAYING FROM WRONG PLACE

DEFINITIONS

All defined terms are in *italics* and are listed alphabetically in the Definitions section – see pages 6–15.

See **incident** involving Rule 20-1 on page 85

20-1. LIFTING AND MARKING
A ball to be lifted under the *Rules* may be lifted by the player, his *partner* or another person authorised by the player. In any such case, the player is responsible for any breach of the *Rules*.

The position of the ball must be marked before it is lifted under a *Rule* that requires it to be replaced. If it is not marked, **the player incurs a penalty of one stroke** and the ball must be replaced. If it is not replaced, **the player incurs the general penalty for breach of this Rule** but there is no additional penalty under Rule 20-1.

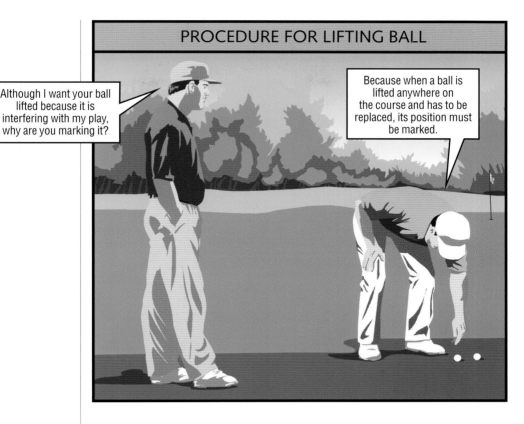

If a ball or ball-marker is accidentally *moved* in the process of lifting the ball under a *Rule* or marking its position, the ball or ball-marker must be replaced. There is no penalty provided the movement of the ball or ball-marker is directly attributable to the specific act of marking the position of or lifting the ball. Otherwise, **the player incurs a penalty of one stroke** under this Rule or Rule 18-2a.

Exception: If a player incurs a penalty for failing to act in accordance with Rule 5-3 or 12-2, there is no additional penalty under Rule 20-1.

Note: The position of a ball to be lifted should be marked by placing a ball-marker, a small coin or other similar object immediately behind the ball. If the ball-marker interferes with the play, *stance* or *stroke* of another player, it should be placed one or more clubhead-lengths to one side.

20-2. DROPPING AND RE-DROPPING
a. By Whom and How

See **incident** involving Rule 20-2a on page 85

A ball to be dropped under the *Rules* must be dropped by the player himself. He must stand erect, hold the ball at shoulder height and arm's length and drop it. If a ball is dropped by any other person or in any other manner and the error is not corrected as provided in Rule 20-6, **the player incurs a penalty of one stroke**.

If the ball touches the player, his *partner*, either of their *caddies* or their *equipment* before or after it strikes a part of the *course*, the ball must be re-dropped, without penalty. There is no limit to the number of times a ball must be re-dropped in these circumstances.

(Taking action to influence position or movement of ball – see Rule 1-2)

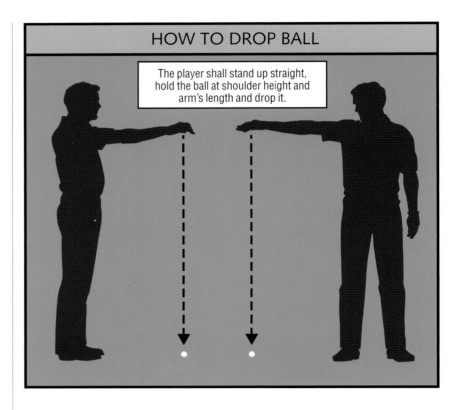

HOW TO DROP BALL

The player shall stand up straight, hold the ball at shoulder height and arm's length and drop it.

b. Where to Drop

When a ball is to be dropped as near as possible to a specific spot, it must be dropped not nearer the *hole* than the specific spot which, if it is not precisely known to the player, must be estimated.

A ball when dropped must first strike a part of the *course* where the applicable *Rule* requires it to be dropped. If it is not so dropped, Rules 20-6 and -7 apply.

c. When to Re-Drop

See **incident** involving Rule 20-2c on page 85

A dropped ball must be re-dropped without penalty if it:

(i)   rolls into and comes to rest in a *hazard*;

(ii)   rolls out of and comes to rest outside a *hazard*;

(iii)   rolls onto and comes to rest on a *putting green*;

(iv)   rolls and comes to rest *out of bounds*;

(v)   rolls to and comes to rest in a position where there is interference by the condition from which relief was taken under Rule 24-2b (immovable obstruction), Rule 25-1 (abnormal ground conditions), Rule 25-3 (wrong putting green) or a Local Rule (Rule 33-8a), or rolls back into the pitch-mark from which it was lifted under Rule 25-2 (embedded ball);

(vi)   rolls and comes to rest more than two club-lengths from where it first struck a part of the *course*; or

(vii)   rolls and comes to rest nearer the *hole* than:

(a) its original position or estimated position (see Rule 20-2b) unless otherwise permitted by the *Rules*; or

(b) the *nearest point of relief* or maximum available relief (Rule 24-2, 25-1 or 25-3); or

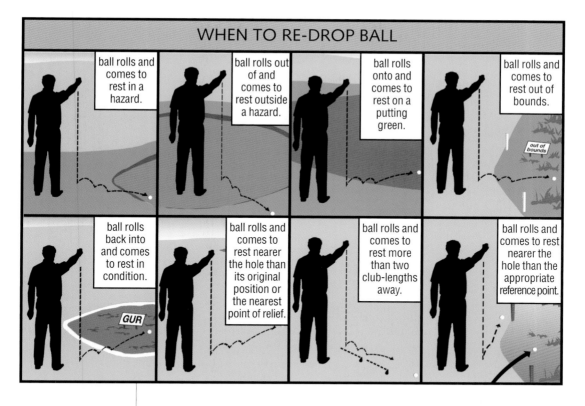

(c) the point where the original ball last crossed the margin of the *water hazard* or *lateral water hazard* (Rule 26-1).

If the ball when re-dropped rolls into any position listed above, it must be placed as near as possible to the spot where it first struck a part of the *course* when re-dropped.

If a ball to be re-dropped or placed under this Rule is not immediately recoverable, another ball may be *substituted*.

Note: If a ball when dropped or re-dropped comes to rest and subsequently *moves*, the ball must be played as it lies, unless the provisions of any other *Rule* apply.

20-3. PLACING AND REPLACING
a. By Whom and Where

A ball to be placed under the *Rules* must be placed by the player or his *partner*. If a ball is to be replaced, the player, his *partner* or the person who lifted or *moved* it must place it on the spot from which it was lifted or *moved*. In any such case, the player is responsible for any breach of the *Rules*.

If a ball or ball-marker is accidentally *moved* in the process of placing or replacing the ball, the ball or ball-marker must be replaced. There is no penalty provided the movement of the ball or ball-marker is directly attributable to the specific act of placing or replacing the ball or removing the ball-marker. Otherwise, **the player incurs a *penalty stroke*** under Rule 18-2a or 20-1.

b. Lie of Ball to be Placed or Replaced Altered

If the original lie of a ball to be placed or replaced has been altered:

81

(i) except in a *hazard*, the ball must be placed in the nearest lie most similar to the original lie that is not more than one club-length from the original lie, not nearer the *hole* and not in a *hazard*;

(ii) in a *water hazard*, the ball must be placed in accordance with Clause (i) above, except that the ball must be placed in the *water hazard*;

(iii) in a *bunker*, the original lie must be re-created as nearly as possible and the ball must be placed in that lie.

c. Spot Not Determinable

See **incident** involving Rule 20-3c on page 115–116

If it is impossible to determine the spot where the ball is to be placed or replaced:

(i) *through the green*, the ball must be dropped as near as possible to the place where it lay but not in a *hazard* or on a *putting green*;

(ii) in a *hazard*, the ball must be dropped in the *hazard* as near as possible to the place where it lay;

(iii) on the *putting green*, the ball must be placed as near as possible to the place where it lay but not in a *hazard*.

Exception: When resuming play (Rule 6-8d), if the spot where the ball is to be placed is impossible to determine, it must be estimated and the ball placed on the estimated spot.

d. Ball Fails to Come to Rest on Spot

See **incident** involving Rule 20-3d on page 85

If a ball when placed fails to come to rest on the spot on which it was placed, there is no penalty and the ball must be replaced. If it still fails to come to rest on that spot:

(i) except in a *hazard*, it must be placed at the nearest spot where it can be placed at rest that is not nearer the *hole* and not in a *hazard*;

(ii) in a *hazard*, it must be placed in the *hazard* at the nearest spot where it can be placed at rest that is not nearer the *hole*.

If a ball when placed comes to rest on the spot on which it is placed, and it subsequently *moves*, there is no penalty and the ball must be played as it lies, unless the provisions of any other *Rule* apply.

PENALTY FOR BREACH OF RULE 20-1, 20-2 or 20-3:

Match play – Loss of hole; Stroke play – Two strokes.

20-4. WHEN BALL DROPPED OR PLACED IS IN PLAY

If the player's *ball in play* has been lifted, it is again in play when dropped or placed.

A *substituted ball* becomes the *ball in play* when it has been dropped or placed.

(Ball incorrectly substituted – see Rule 15-2)

(Lifting ball incorrectly substituted, dropped or placed – see Rule 20-6)

20-5. MAKING NEXT STROKE FROM WHERE PREVIOUS STROKE MADE

When a player elects or is required to make his next *stroke* from where a previous *stroke* was made, he must proceed as follows:

a. **On the Teeing Ground:** The ball to be played must be played from within the *teeing ground*. It may be played from anywhere within the *teeing ground* and may be teed.

b. **Through the Green and in a Hazard:** The ball to be played must be dropped.

c. **On the Putting Green:** The ball to be played must be placed.

PENALTY FOR BREACH OF RULE 20-5:

Match play – Loss of hole; Stroke play – Two strokes.

20-6. LIFTING BALL INCORRECTLY SUBSTITUTED, DROPPED OR PLACED

A ball incorrectly *substituted*, dropped or placed in a wrong place or otherwise not in accordance with the *Rules* but not played may be lifted, without penalty, and the player must then proceed correctly.

20-7. PLAYING FROM WRONG PLACE
a. General
A player has played from a wrong place if he makes a *stroke* with his *ball in play*:
(i)   on a part of the *course* where the *Rules* do not permit a *stroke* to be played or a ball to be dropped or placed; or
(ii) when the *Rules* require a dropped ball to be re-dropped or a *moved* ball to be replaced.
Note: For a ball played from outside the *teeing ground* or from a wrong *teeing ground* – see Rule 11-4.

b. Match Play
If a player makes a *stroke* from a wrong place, **he loses the hole**.

c. Stroke Play
If a *competitor* makes a *stroke* from a wrong place, **he incurs a penalty of two strokes under the applicable Rule**. He must play out the hole with the ball played from the wrong place, without correcting his error, provided he has not committed a serious breach (see Note 1).

If a *competitor* becomes aware that he has played from a wrong place and believes that he may have committed a serious breach, he must, before making a *stroke* on the next *teeing ground*, play out the hole with a second ball dropped or placed in accordance with the *Rules*. If the hole being played is

PLAYING FROM WRONG PLACE

If a player moves his ball-marker a putter head length to one side, he must remember to put it back before he putts. Otherwise, the player will be penalised for playing from a wrong place.

the last hole of the round, he must declare, before leaving the *putting green*, that he will play out the hole with a second ball dropped or placed in accordance with the *Rules*.

The *competitor* must report the facts to the *Committee* before returning his score card; if he fails to do so, **he is disqualified**. The *Committee* must determine whether the *competitor* has committed a serious breach of the applicable *Rule*. If he has, the score with the second ball counts and **the competitor must add two penalty strokes** to his score with that ball. If the *competitor* has committed a serious breach and has failed to correct it as outlined above, **he is disqualified**.

Note 1: A *competitor* is deemed to have committed a serious breach of the applicable *Rule* if the *Committee* considers he has gained a significant advantage as a result of playing from a wrong place.

Note 2: If a *competitor* plays a second ball under Rule 20-7c and it is ruled not to count, *strokes* made with that ball and *penalty strokes* incurred solely by playing that ball are disregarded. If the second ball is ruled to count, the *stroke* made from the wrong place and any *strokes* subsequently taken with the original ball including *penalty strokes* incurred solely by playing that ball are disregarded.

RULE 20 INCIDENTS

While playing the par-5 2nd hole at Augusta in the third round of the 1995 Masters, Nick Faldo hit his drive into the pine trees, his ball coming to rest in a ditch marked as a lateral water hazard. Faldo elected to follow the procedure prescribed in Rule 26-1c by dropping his ball within two club-lengths of where the ball last crossed the margin of the hazard.

On dropping, the ball struck Faldo's foot and rolled back into the hazard. Unsure of the correct procedure, Faldo called for a Rules official. Rule 20-2a provides that in such a case where a dropped ball touches the player before or after it strikes part of the course, the ball shall be re-dropped, without penalty. There is no limit to the number of times a ball shall be re-dropped in such circumstances, as it is effectively a "no drop". Therefore, when Faldo's second attempt at dropping the ball rolled into the hazard he was required to drop the ball a third time. When re-dropped the ball rolled and came to rest in the hazard again, so Faldo then had to place the ball on the spot where it first struck the ground when re-dropped.

In the 1999 Greg Norman Holden International at The Lakes Golf Club in Sydney, Bernhard Langer, needing a par 3 at the final hole to win missed the green and then played a poor chip to leave himself a 25 foot putt for his par. Having marked the position of his ball he lifted it and passed to his caddie for cleaning. When it was Langer's turn to putt he bent down to replace his ball but prior to doing so, for some inexplicable reason, he picked up his marker, at which point he stood up with both marker and ball in his hand. Having been penalised one stroke under Rule 20-1 Langer replaced his marker as near as possible to its original position, replaced the ball and proceeded to take three putts and lose the Tournament by two strokes.

RULE  CLEANING BALL

DEFINITIONS

See **incident** involving Rule 21 below

All defined terms are in *italics* and are listed alphabetically in the Definitions section – see pages 6–15.

A ball on the *putting green* may be cleaned when lifted under Rule 16-1b. Elsewhere, a ball may be cleaned when lifted except when it has been lifted:

a. To determine if it is unfit for play (Rule 5-3);

b. For identification (Rule 12-2), in which case it may be cleaned only to the extent necessary for identification; or

c. Because it is assisting or interfering with play (Rule 22).

If a player cleans his ball during play of a hole except as provided in this Rule, **he incurs a penalty of one stroke** and the ball, if lifted, must be replaced.

If a player who is required to replace a ball fails to do so, **he incurs the penalty** for breach of Rule 20-3a, but there is no additional penalty under Rule 21.

Exception: If a player incurs a penalty for failing to act in accordance with Rule 5-3, 12-2 or 22, there is no additional penalty under Rule 21.

RULE 21 INCIDENT

During the 1999 U.S. Open at Pinehurst – six holes after the incident described under Rule 22 (see page 86) – Scott Hoch holed his bunker shot at the par-4 12th. During the clamour, the walking Rules official looked up to see two senior Rules officials motioning him to come over.

The senior officials reported that a spectator had alleged that Hoch's ball was mistakenly cleaned when lifted for interference at the 6th hole. Rule 22 permits the lifting of a ball that interferes with or assists the play of another player but under such circumstances, except on the putting green, the ball may not be cleaned when lifted under Rule 22.

The senior officials asked the walking official if he could confirm whether Hoch's ball had been cleaned when lifted from the greenside rough. The walking official stated that his attention had been primarily focused on the lifting and replacing procedures and he was unaware of any cleaning breach.

It was decided to ask Hoch about the incident after he finished the round but before he returned his score card. When the inquiry was made Hoch replied that he did not recall since the incident had occurred two hours before. Hoch's caddie also said he did not recall. Parnevik and Jones said they were not watching and could not say.

Since there was no evidence to the contrary, Hoch was found to have acted properly and he began the second round just four shots off the lead.

RULE 22

BALL ASSISTING OR INTERFERING WITH PLAY

DEFINITIONS

All defined terms are in *italics* and are listed alphabetically in the Definitions section – see pages 6–15.

See **incident** involving Rule 22 on page 88

22-1. BALL ASSISTING PLAY

Except when a ball is in motion, if a player considers that a ball might assist any other player, he may:

a. lift the ball if it is his ball; or

b. have any other ball lifted.

A ball lifted under this Rule must be replaced (see Rule 20-3). The ball must not be cleaned unless it lies on the *putting green* (see Rule 21).

In stroke play, a player required to lift his ball may play first rather than lift the ball.

In stroke play, if the *Committee* determines that *competitors* have agreed not to lift a ball that might assist any other player, **they are disqualified**.

22-2. BALL INTERFERING WITH PLAY

Except when a ball is in motion, if a player considers that the ball of another player might interfere with his play, he may have it lifted.

A ball lifted under this Rule must be replaced (see Rule 20-3). The ball must not be cleaned unless it lies on the *putting green* (see Rule 21).

In stroke play, a player required to lift his ball may play first rather than lift the ball.

BALL INTERFERING WITH OR ASSISTING PLAY

Note: Except on the *putting green*, a player may not lift his ball solely because he considers that it might interfere with the play of another player. If a player lifts his ball without being asked to do so, **he incurs a penalty of one stroke** for a breach of Rule 18-2a, but there is no additional penalty under Rule 22.

PENALTY FOR BREACH OF RULE:
Match play – Loss of hole; Stroke play – Two strokes.

RULE 22 INCIDENT

Because golf is played on the largest playing field of any sport, it's rare for one ball to touch another.

However, Jesper Parnevik and Scott Hoch found themselves in such a predicament just off the 6th green at Pinehurst No.2 during the 1999 U.S. Open. Fortunately, the procedure in such a situation is concise.

The shortest Rule in the book, Rule 22 allows any player to lift his ball if he believes it will assist another player, or have any ball lifted that might interfere with his play or assist any other player. Except on the putting green, a ball lifted under this Rule may not be cleaned.

Hoch and Parnevik both played just to the left side of the green at this 222-yard par 3. Upon arriving at the green, they found that the balls were touching one another and lay about three inches off the fringe in the Bermuda grass rough. Both balls were held slightly off the ground by the stiff nature of the grass. Because Hoch's ball was closer to the hole, it was necessary that it be lifted in order for Parnevik to play his shot.

When Hoch lifted his ball, Parnevik's moved an inch closer to the hole. Under a Rules official's watchful eye, Parnevik attempted to replace his ball in its original location. However, the supporting nature of the Bermuda grass could not be reintroduced and Parnevik's ball sunk a littler deeper into the rough than its original position. Under the Rules, it doesn't matter if the movement is vertical or horizontal. The ball could not be replaced in its original position so that it would remain at rest.

Rule 20-3d covers such a situation by stating that if a ball, when placed or replaced, fails to come to rest on that spot it shall be replaced. If it again fails to remain at rest, it must be placed at the nearest spot where it can be placed at rest which is not nearer the hole and not in a hazard.

Therefore, Parnevik found another spot that was nearest to the original position where the ball would remain at rest. He chipped onto the green and in doing so altered Hoch's lie.

In this case, Hoch was entitled to the lie that his shot gave him. Since his lie had been altered, he found the nearest lie most similar to and within one club-length of his original lie placed his ball at that spot. Then he chipped in for a birdie two.

All of this was under the discerning eyes of both the walking Rules official and a Rules rover who was monitoring the group's pace of play. Parnevik and Jones finished the hole and the group went to the 7th tee. See Rule 21 for a continuation of this incident.

A player is entitled to remove any loose impediment without penalty, except when both the loose impediment and the player's ball lie in or touch the same hazard.

RULE **23**

LOOSE IMPEDIMENTS

DEFINITIONS

All defined terms are in *italics* and are listed alphabetically in the Definitions section – see pages 6–15.

See **incident**
involving Rule 23-1
on page 90

23-1. RELIEF

Except when both the *loose impediment* and the ball lie in or touch the same *hazard*, any *loose impediment* may be removed without penalty.

If the ball lies anywhere other than on the *putting green* and the removal of a *loose impediment* by the player causes the ball to *move*, Rule 18-2a applies.

On the *putting green*, if the ball or ball-marker *moves* in the process of the player removing any *loose impediment*, the ball or ball-marker must be replaced. There is no penalty provided the movement of the ball or ball-marker is directly attributable to the removal of the *loose impediment*. Otherwise, if the player causes the ball to *move*, **he incurs a penalty of one**

Loose impediments are natural objects that come in all shapes and sizes. At the 1999 Phoenix Open, Tiger Woods learned that a player can receive assistance in removing a large loose impediment. Details of this incident can be reviewed on page 90.

stroke under Rule 18-2a.

When a ball is in motion, a *loose impediment* that might influence the movement of the ball must not be removed.

Note: If the ball lies in a *hazard*, the player must not touch or move any *loose impediment* lying in or touching the same *hazard* – see Rule 13-4c.

PENALTY FOR BREACH OF RULE:

Match play – Loss of hole; Stroke play – Two strokes.

(Searching for ball in hazard – see Rule 12-1)

(Touching line of putt – see Rule 16-1a)

RULE 23 INCIDENT

The Rules of Golf permitted Tiger Woods to gain assistance from his substantial gallery in moving a loose impediment during the 1999 Phoenix Open.

During the final round, Woods' drive from the 13th tee travelled 360 yards before finishing in the desert just off the left side of the fairway. The ball stopped about two feet directly behind a boulder that was roughly four feet wide, two feet high and two feet thick. The rock was too heavy for Woods to move by himself, and his ball was too close to it to play over or around. Without moving the rock, his best option would have been to play sideways into the fairway.

With 225 yards to the putting green, Woods was not inclined to pitch out without first knowing what his options were with regard to the rock.

A PGA Tour Rules official appeared at the scene. With a glimmer of a smile on his face, Woods kicked the rock and asked, "... It's not a pebble but is it a loose impediment?"

The definition within the Rules of Golf states that loose impediments are natural objects that are not fixed or growing, not solidly embedded and do not adhere to the ball. There is no reference to size or weight.

Decision 23-1/2 states that stones of any size are loose impediments and may be removed, as long as they are not solidly embedded and their removal does not unduly delay play.

The official replied, "It's readily movable if you have people who can move it real quick."

"Really?" Woods responded to the revelation quietly.

Then the official added in an inquiring tone, "But it kind of looks embedded to me."

"It's embedded?" Woods asked as they both stepped back to look.

The official decided the stone was just lying on the desert floor and was not solidly embedded. He also knew that Decision 23-1/3 specifically permits spectators, caddies, fellow-competitors, essentially anyone to assist in removing a large loose impediment.

Several men rolled the stone out of Woods' line of play as others watched and cheered. Following the removal, Woods shook each man's hand and then played his shot directly toward the green, where it finished in the bunker to the right of the green.

RULE **24** | OBSTRUCTIONS

DEFINITIONS

All defined terms are in *italics* and are listed alphabetically in the Definitions section – see pages 6–15.

See **incident** involving Rule 24-1 on page 97–98

24-1. MOVABLE OBSTRUCTION

A player may take relief without penalty from a movable *obstruction* as follows:

a. If the ball does not lie in or on the *obstruction*, the *obstruction* may be removed. If the ball *moves*, it must be replaced, and there is no penalty provided that the movement of the ball is directly attributable to the removal of the *obstruction*. Otherwise, Rule 18-2a applies.

b. If the ball lies in or on the *obstruction*, the ball may be lifted, and the *obstruction* removed. The ball must *through the green* or in a *hazard* be dropped, or on the *putting green* be placed, as near as possible to the spot directly under the place where the ball lay in or on the *obstruction*, but not nearer the *hole*.

The ball may be cleaned when lifted under this Rule.

When a ball is in motion, an *obstruction* that might influence the movement of the ball, other than an attended *flagstick* or *equipment* of the players, must not be removed.

(Exerting influence on ball – see Rule 1-2)

Note: If a ball to be dropped or placed under this Rule is not immediately recoverable, another ball may be *substituted*.

BALL AGAINST RAKE ROLLS INTO BUNKER WHEN RAKE REMOVED

If I move the rake my ball is likely to roll into the bunker. If it does, may I replace it?

Yes, and if it will not come to rest on the correct spot when replaced, you may place it at the nearest spot, not nearer the hole nor in the bunker, where it can be placed at rest.

24-2. IMMOVABLE OBSTRUCTION

a. Interference

Interference by an immovable *obstruction* occurs when a ball lies in or on the *obstruction*, or when the *obstruction* interferes with the player's *stance* or the area of his intended swing. If the player's ball lies on the *putting green*, interference also occurs if an immovable *obstruction* on the *putting green* intervenes on his *line of putt*. Otherwise, intervention on the *line of play* is not, of itself, interference under this Rule.

b. Relief

Except when the ball is in a *water hazard* or a *lateral water hazard*, a player may take relief from interference by an immovable *obstruction* as follows:

See **incidents** involving Rule 24-2b on page 97–99

(i) **Through the Green:** If the ball lies *through the green*, the player must lift the ball and drop it without penalty within one club-length of and not nearer the *hole* than the *nearest point of relief*. The *nearest point of relief* must not be in a *hazard* or on a *putting green*. When the ball is dropped within one club-length of the *nearest point of relief*, the ball must first strike a part of the *course* at a spot that avoids interference by the immovable *obstruction* and is not in a *hazard* and not on a *putting green*.

(ii) **In a Bunker:** If the ball is in a *bunker*, the player must lift the ball and drop it either:

(a) Without penalty, in accordance with Clause (i) above, except that the *nearest point of relief* must be in the *bunker* and the ball must be dropped in the *bunker*; or

(b) **Under penalty of one stroke**, outside the *bunker* keeping the point where the ball lay directly between the *hole* and the spot on which the ball is dropped, with no limit to how far behind the *bunker* the ball may be dropped.

NEAREST POINT OF RELIEF

I am trying to determine my nearest point of relief from this immovable obstruction. Am I doing it correctly?

Yes. You have taken the club with which you wish to play the stroke and you are simulating the address position for the stroke. In so doing you will identify the nearest point of relief with reference to where the ball lies.

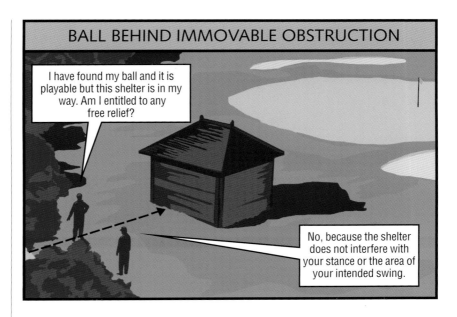

(iii) **On the Putting Green:** If the ball lies on the *putting green*, the player must lift the ball and place it without penalty at the *nearest point of relief* that is not in a *hazard*. The *nearest point of relief* may be off the *putting green*.

(iv) **On the Teeing Ground:** If the ball lies on the *teeing ground*, the player must lift the ball and drop it without penalty in accordance with Clause (i) above.

The ball may be cleaned when lifted under this Rule.

(Ball rolling to a position where there is interference by the condition from which relief was taken – see Rule 20-2c(v))

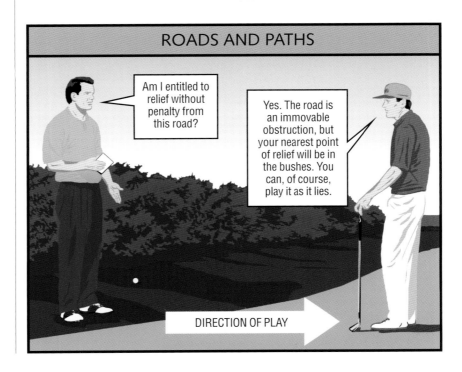

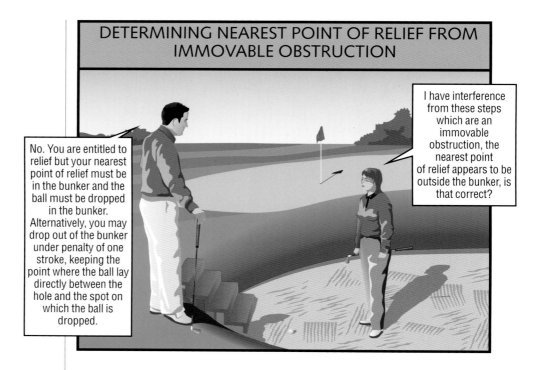

Exception: A player may not take relief under this Rule if (a) it is clearly unreasonable for him to make a *stroke* because of interference by anything other than an immovable *obstruction* or (b) interference by an immovable *obstruction* would occur only through use of an unnecessarily abnormal *stance*, swing or direction of play.

Note 1: If a ball is in a *water hazard* (including a *lateral water hazard*), the player may not take relief from interference by an immovable *obstruction*. The player must play the ball as it lies or proceed under Rule 26-1.

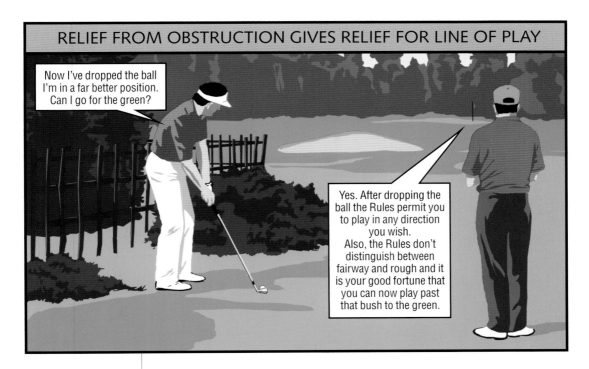

Note 2: If a ball to be dropped or placed under this Rule is not immediately recoverable, another ball may be *substituted*.

Note 3: The *Committee* may make a Local Rule stating that the player must determine the *nearest point of relief* without crossing over, through or under the *obstruction*.

24-3. BALL LOST IN OBSTRUCTION

It is a question of fact whether a ball *lost* after having been struck toward an

After David Frost was denied relief from the road to the left of the 2nd hole at Carnoustie he played his ball onto the road and then took relief under Rule 24-2 – see incident on page 97.

obstruction is *lost* in the *obstruction*. In order to treat the ball as *lost* in the *obstruction*, there must be reasonable evidence to that effect. In the absence of such evidence, the ball must be treated as a *lost ball* and Rule 27 applies.

a. Ball Lost in Movable Obstruction

If a ball is *lost* in a movable obstruction, a player may, without penalty, remove the *obstruction* and must *through the green* or in a *hazard* drop a ball, or on the *putting green* place a ball, as near as possible to the spot directly under the place where the ball last crossed the outermost limits of the movable *obstruction*, but not nearer the *hole*.

b. Ball Lost in Immovable Obstruction

If a ball is *lost* in an immovable *obstruction*, the spot where the ball last crossed the outermost limits of the *obstruction* must be determined and, for the purpose of applying this Rule, the ball is deemed to lie at this spot and the player may take relief as follows:

(i)   **Through the Green:** If the ball last crossed the outermost limits of the immovable *obstruction* at a spot *through the green*, the player may *substitute* another ball without penalty and take relief as prescribed in Rule 24-2b(i).

(ii) **In a Bunker:** If the ball last crossed the outermost limits of the immovable *obstruction* at a spot in a *bunker*, the player may *substitute* another ball without penalty and take relief as prescribed in Rule 24-2b(ii).

(iii) **In a Water Hazard (including a Lateral Water Hazard):** If the ball last crossed the outermost limits of the immovable *obstruction* at a spot in a *water hazard*, the player is not entitled to relief without penalty. The player must proceed under Rule 26-1.

(iv) **On the Putting Green:** If the ball last crossed the outermost limits of the immovable *obstruction* at a spot on the *putting green*, the player may *substitute* another ball without penalty and take relief as prescribed in Rule 24-2b(iii).

PENALTY FOR BREACH OF RULE:

Match play – Loss of hole; Stroke play – Two strokes.

RULE 24 INCIDENTS

Since 1744, the basic tenets of the Rules have been to play the course as you find it, the ball as it lies and, if you are unsure of the proper procedure, to do what is fair. Harry Bradshaw held true to this spirit at the 1949 British Open.

Having shot a stunning first round 68 over Royal St. George's, Bradshaw was tied with Roberto De Vicenzo one stroke behind Jimmy Adams. However, playing the 5th hole during the second round, Bradshaw's ball rolled into a discarded beer bottle from which the neck had been broken.

Rather than requesting a ruling for the relief to which he was entitled, Bradshaw determined on his own that he must play the ball as it lay. He took out his sand wedge and made a swing, which shattered the bottle and moved the ball slightly forward. He took a double bogey six.

The result of his playing out of this movable obstruction was that Bradshaw ultimately tied Bobby Locke of South Africa at 283. In the resulting 36-hole play-off, Locke scored 136 to Bradshaw's 147, to win the first of Locke's four Open Championships.

Under Rule 24-1, because Bradshaw's ball was in a movable obstruction, the ball could have been lifted and cleaned without penalty, the bottle removed and the ball dropped as nearly as possible to the spot directly under the place where the ball lay when it was in the bottle.

In choosing to take relief from an immovable obstruction, the ball must be dropped in a place that avoids interference by the immovable obstruction. Full relief must be taken. Payne Stewart learned this lesson in 1993 during the PGA Tours annual stop in San Diego.

In taking relief from a cart path, Stewart dropped his ball in a place where, after taking his stance, the heel of his right shoe was still on the cart path from which he was taking relief. The television broadcast showed the breach clearly and Stewart was penalised two strokes for not taking complete relief from the immovable obstruction.

The Exception to Rule 24-2 states clearly that a player may not obtain relief under this Rule if interference would only occur through the use of an abnormal stance, swing or direction of play. This is one of the places in the Rules where a Referee's judgment is called upon, as David Frost learned during the final round of the 1999 Open Championship at Carnoustie.

Playing with Justin Leonard in the penultimate group, Frost's drive at the second hole was a low hook into the high rough. Near the area where he would stand to play the ball was a road. Frost argued to the attending Rules official that in order to play the ball, which was below his feet, he would have to widen his stance to such an extent that he would be standing on the road and, therefore, he was entitled to relief from an immovable obstruction.

The referee did not accept the argument and told Frost that such a play was not reasonable. It was the official's judgment that had the road not been there, Frost would not have used a stance that would place his left foot on the road. With the final pairing waiting on the tee, time ticked away as confirmation of the official's decision was requested over the radio. It was deemed final, and Frost played the ball as it lay. His shot from this awkward lie came to rest on the road, from where he was then granted relief under Rule 24-2.

In such a situation, the Rules official must consider how the player would attempt the shot if the obstruction in question were not present. In a stroke play situation such as this one, the Rules are there to protect the field and prevent an unfair advantage of one player over all the others.

When the Committee declares an obstruction an integral part of the golf course, it eliminates any argument because there is no free relief. The most famous example of this is on the Road Hole at the Old

When the Committee declares an immovable obstruction to be an integral part of the course, in this case the road behind the 17th green of the Old Course at St Andrews, relief without penalty is not available.

Course in St. Andrews. When a ball lies on the road immediately to the right of the green, it must be played as it lies. As the name of the hole suggests, the road has always been the most important element of the 17th hole, and to allow relief would eliminate one of its essential obstacles. Thus, it is an integral part of the golf course.

RULE 25 ABNORMAL GROUND CONDITIONS, EMBEDDED BALL AND WRONG PUTTING GREEN

DEFINITIONS All defined terms are in *italics* and are listed alphabetically in the Definitions section – see pages 6–15.

25-1. ABNORMAL GROUND CONDITIONS
a. Interference
Interference by an *abnormal ground condition* occurs when a ball lies in or touches the condition or when the condition interferes with the player's *stance* or the area of his intended swing. If the player's ball lies on the *putting green*, interference also occurs if an *abnormal ground condition* on the *putting green* intervenes on his *line of putt*. Otherwise, intervention on the *line of play* is not, of itself, interference under this Rule.

Note: The *Committee* may make a Local Rule denying the player relief from interference with his *stance* by an *abnormal ground condition*.

b. Relief
Except when the ball is in a *water hazard* or a *lateral water hazard*, a player may take relief from interference by an *abnormal ground condition* as follows:

See **incident** involving Rule 25-1b on page 106

A fallen tree still attached to its stump is not ground under repair., but it can be so declared by the Committee.

A rut made by a tractor is not ground under repair, but the Committee would be justified in declaring a deep rut to be ground under repair.

(i) **Through the Green:** If the ball lies *through the green*, the player must lift the ball and drop it without penalty within one club-length of and not nearer the *hole* than the *nearest point of relief*. The *nearest point of relief* must not be in a *hazard* or on a *putting green*. When the ball is dropped within one club-length of the *nearest point of relief*, the ball must first strike a part of the *course* at a spot that avoids interference by the condition and is not in a *hazard* and not on a *putting green*.

(ii) **In a Bunker:** If the ball is in a *bunker*, the player must lift the ball and drop it either:

(a) Without penalty, in accordance with Clause (i) above, except that the *nearest point of relief* must be in the *bunker* and the ball must be dropped in the *bunker*, or if complete relief is impossible, as near as

AREAS REQUIRING PRESERVATION

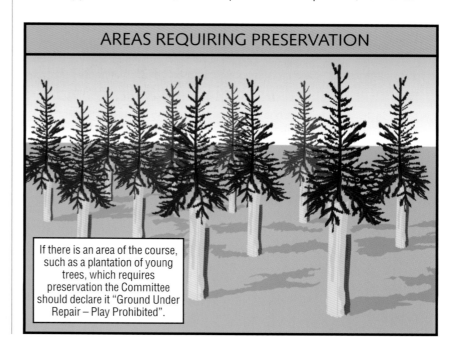

If there is an area of the course, such as a plantation of young trees, which requires preservation the Committee should declare it "Ground Under Repair – Play Prohibited".

possible to the spot where the ball lay, but not nearer the *hole*, on a part of the *course* in the *bunker* that affords maximum available relief from the condition; or

(b) **Under penalty of one stroke**, outside the *bunker* keeping the point where the ball lay directly between the *hole* and the spot on which the ball is dropped, with no limit to how far behind the *bunker* the ball may be dropped.

(iii) **On the Putting Green:** If the ball lies on the *putting green*, the player must lift the ball and place it without penalty at the *nearest point of relief* that is not in a *hazard*, or if complete relief is impossible, at the nearest position to where it lay that affords maximum available relief from the condition, but not nearer the *hole* and not in a *hazard*. The *nearest point of relief* or maximum available relief may be off the *putting green*.

(iv) **On the Teeing Ground:** If the ball lies on the *teeing ground*, the player must lift the ball and drop it without penalty in accordance with Clause (i) above.

The ball may be cleaned when lifted under Rule 25-1b.

(Ball rolling to a position where there is interference by the condition from which relief was taken – see Rule 20-2c(v))

Exception: A player may not take relief under this Rule if (a) it is clearly unreasonable for him to make a *stroke* because of interference by anything other than an *abnormal ground condition* or (b) interference by an *abnormal ground condition* would occur only through use of an unnecessarily abnormal *stance*, swing or direction of play.

Note 1: If a ball is in a *water hazard* (including a *lateral water hazard*), the player is not entitled to relief without penalty from interference by an *abnormal ground condition*. The player must play the ball as it lies (unless prohibited by Local Rule) or proceed under Rule 26-1.

Note 2: If a ball to be dropped or placed under this Rule is not immediately recoverable, another ball may be *substituted*.

c. Ball Lost

See **incident** involving Rule 25-1c on page 106–107

It is a question of fact whether a ball *lost* after having been struck toward an *abnormal ground condition* is *lost* in such condition. In order to treat the ball as *lost* in the *abnormal ground condition*, there must be reasonable evidence to that effect. In the absence of such evidence, the ball must be treated as a *lost ball* and Rule 27 applies.

If a ball is *lost* in an *abnormal ground condition*, the spot where the ball last crossed the outermost limits of the condition must be determined and, for the purpose of applying this Rule, the ball is deemed to lie at this spot and the player may take relief as follows:

(i) **Through the Green:** If the ball last crossed the outermost limits of the *abnormal ground condition* at a spot *through the green*, the player may *substitute* another ball without penalty and take relief as prescribed in Rule 25-1b(i).

(ii) **In a Bunker:** If the ball last crossed the outermost limits of the *abnormal ground condition* at a spot in a *bunker*, the player may *substitute* another ball without penalty and take relief as prescribed in Rule 25-1b(ii).

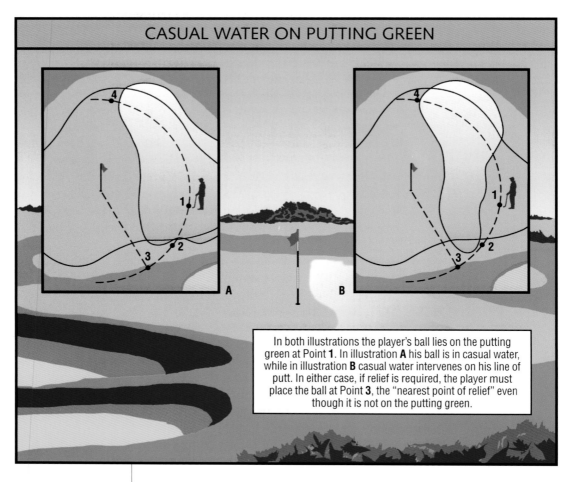

CASUAL WATER ON PUTTING GREEN

In both illustrations the player's ball lies on the putting green at Point **1**. In illustration **A** his ball is in casual water, while in illustration **B** casual water intervenes on his line of putt. In either case, if relief is required, the player must place the ball at Point **3**, the "nearest point of relief" even though it is not on the putting green.

BALL CLOSE TO CASUAL WATER: LEFT HANDED STROKE NOT REASONABLE

BALL CLOSE TO CASUAL WATER: LEFT HANDED STROKE REASONABLE

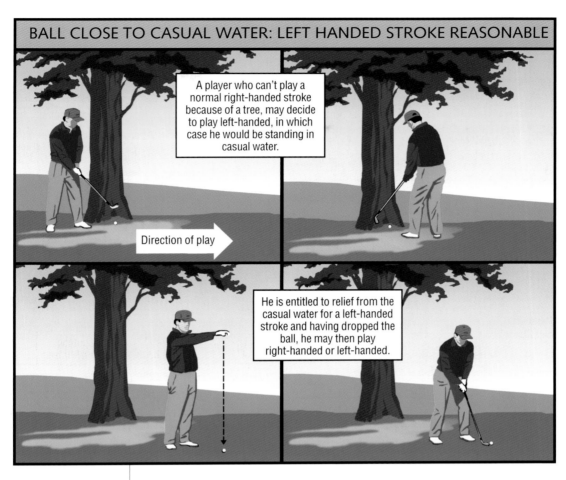

BALL IN CASUAL WATER IN BUNKER

(iii) **In a Water Hazard (including a Lateral Water Hazard):** If the ball last crossed the outermost limits of the *abnormal ground condition* at a spot in a *water hazard*, the player is not entitled to relief without penalty. The player must proceed under Rule 26-1.

(iv) **On the Putting Green:** If the ball last crossed the outermost limits of the *abnormal ground condition* at a spot on the *putting green*, the player may *substitute* another ball without penalty and take relief as prescribed in Rule 25-1b(iii).

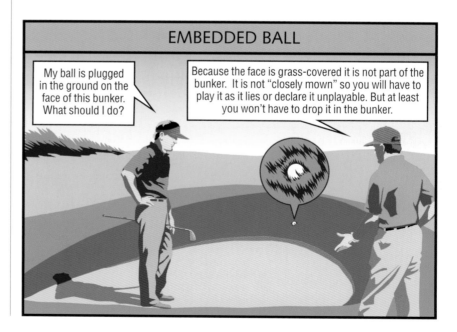

25-2. EMBEDDED BALL

A ball embedded in its own pitch-mark in the ground in any closely-mown area *through the green* may be lifted, cleaned and dropped, without penalty, as near as possible to the spot where it lay but not nearer the *hole*. The ball when dropped must first strike a part of the *course through the green*. "Closely-mown area" means any area of the *course*, including paths through the rough, cut to fairway height or less.

25-3. WRONG PUTTING GREEN
a. Interference

Interference by a *wrong putting green* occurs when a ball is on the *wrong putting green*.

Interference to a player's *stance* or the area of his intended swing is not, of itself, interference under this Rule.

b. Relief

If a player's ball lies on a *wrong putting green*, he must not play the ball as it lies. He must take relief, without penalty, as follows:

The player must lift the ball and drop it within one club-length of and not nearer the hole than the *nearest point of relief*. The *nearest point of relief* must not be in a *hazard* or on a *putting green*. When dropping the ball within one club-length of the *nearest point of relief*, the ball must first strike a part of the *course* at a spot that avoids interference by the *wrong putting green* and is not in a *hazard* and not on a *putting green*. The ball may be cleaned when lifted under this Rule.

PENALTY FOR BREACH OF RULE:
Match play – Loss of hole; Stroke play – Two strokes.

RELIEF FROM A WRONG PUTTING GREEN

RULE 25 INCIDENTS

Tied for the lead going into the final hole of the 1994 Volvo Masters at Valderrama, Severiano Ballesteros pushed his tee shot right and the ball came to rest at the base of a tree, close to a large hole.

The tree was positioned directly between the ball and the hole and Ballesteros, having examined the lie of the ball, decided to call for a Rules official. Ballesteros felt that his ball was lying in earth which had been removed by whatever had dug the hole and, therefore, he thought he may be entitled to free relief from the condition under Rule 25-1. However, as the Rules official was to explain to him, free relief would only be available if the hole had been made by a burrowing animal and the hole or cast was deemed to interfere with the lie of his ball or the area of his intended swing. The official undertook a thorough search for evidence that the hole had been made by a burrowing animal but could find no such evidence and thus denied Ballesteros relief.

The referee's decision was crucial in that if Ballesteros had been entitled to the relief he requested it was apparent that he would have been able to drop a ball in accordance with the Rules, in a position where the tree would no longer have interfered with his line of play and he would have had a clear shot to the green. It transpired that with the relief denied Ballesteros had to chip out sideways and his chance of victory was gone.

During the second round of The Players Championship in 1999, marshals at the 18th green watched Greg Norman's ball roll into a hole made by a burrowing animal. When a ball is lost in an abnormal ground condition, there must be reasonable evidence to that effect. Suspecting that the ball might have gone into the burrowing animal hole is not good enough and, indeed, the Australian started to put his hand into the hole to determine if the ball was there.

"A hole or cast made by a non-burrowing animal is not an abnormal ground condition". Seve Ballesteros is denied relief under Rule 25-1 on the final hole of the 1994 Volvo Masters.

The attending official told Norman that the marshal's statements that they had seen the ball go into the burrowing animal hole constituted reasonable evidence. Therefore, he was entitled to relief without penalty, and it was not necessary to reach into the hole in order to retrieve the ball.

RULE 26 — WATER HAZARDS (INCLUDING LATERAL WATER HAZARDS)

DEFINITIONS

All defined terms are in *italics* and are listed alphabetically in the Definitions section – see pages 6–15.

26-1. RELIEF FOR BALL IN WATER HAZARD

It is a question of fact whether a ball *lost* after having been struck toward a *water hazard* is *lost* inside or outside the *hazard*. In order to treat the ball as *lost* in the *hazard*, there must be reasonable evidence that the ball lodged in it. In the absence of such evidence, the ball must be treated as a *lost ball* and Rule 27 applies.

If a ball is in or is *lost* in a *water hazard* (whether the ball lies in water or not), the player may **under penalty of one stroke**:

a. Play a ball as nearly as possible at the spot from which the original ball was last played (see Rule 20-5); or

b. Drop a ball behind the *water hazard*, keeping the point at which the original ball last crossed the margin of the *water hazard* directly between the *hole* and the spot on which the ball is dropped, with no limit to how far behind the *water hazard* the ball may be dropped; or

c. As additional options available only if the ball last crossed the margin of a *lateral water hazard*, drop a ball outside the *water hazard* within two club-lengths of and not nearer the *hole* than (i) the point where the original ball

See **incident** involving Rule 26-1b on page 111

Jean Van de Velde's difficulty with the Barry Burn at the 72nd hole of the 1999 British Open resulted in a three-way playoff for the championship. See the details of his unfortunate brush with Rule 26-1 in the incident on page 111.

last crossed the margin of the *water hazard* or (ii) a point on the opposite margin of the *water hazard* equidistant from the *hole*.

The ball may be lifted and cleaned when proceeding under this Rule.
(Prohibited actions when ball is in a hazard – see Rule 13-4)
(Ball moving in water in a water hazard – see Rule 14-6)

26-2. BALL PLAYED WITHIN WATER HAZARD
a. Ball Comes to Rest in Same or Another Water Hazard
If a ball played from within a *water hazard* comes to rest in the same or another *water hazard* after the *stroke*, the player may:

(i)   proceed under Rule 26-1a. If, after dropping in the *hazard*, the player elects not to play the dropped ball, he may:

(a) with reference to this *hazard*, proceed under Rule 26-1b, or if applicable Rule 26-1c, adding the **additional penalty of one stroke** prescribed by that Rule; or

(b) **add an additional penalty of one stroke** and play a ball as nearly as possible at the spot from which the last *stroke* from outside a *water hazard* was made (see Rule 20-5); or

(ii)   proceed under Rule 26-1b, or if applicable Rule 26-1c; or

(iii) **under penalty of one stroke**, play a ball as nearly as possible at the spot from which the last *stroke* from outside a *water hazard* was made (see Rule 20-5).

b. Ball Lost or Unplayable Outside Hazard or Out of Bounds
If a ball played from within a *water hazard* is *lost* or declared unplayable outside the *hazard* or is *out of bounds*, the player may, after taking a **penalty of one stroke** under Rule 27-1 or 28a:

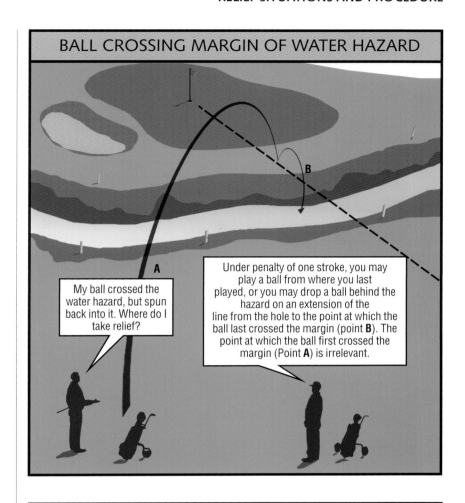

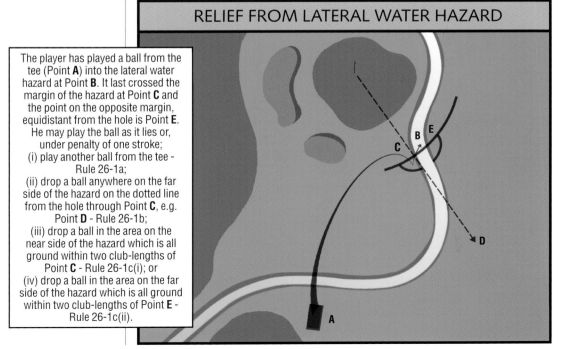

BALL PLAYED FROM WITHIN WATER HAZARD

The player's tee shot at a par 3 hole comes to rest in a water hazard. He plays from the hazard, but fails to get his ball out. He may play the ball as it lies or, under penalty of one stroke:
(i) drop a ball at the spot from which he's just played his second stroke and play again from there;
(ii) drop a ball behind the hazard, anywhere on the dotted line, and play from there; or
(iii) play another ball from the tee.

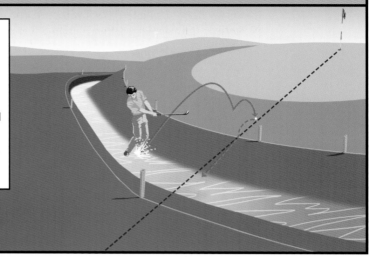

(i)   play a ball as nearly as possible at the spot in the *hazard* from which the original ball was last played (see Rule 20-5); or

(ii)   proceed under Rule 26-1b, or if applicable Rule 26-1c, **adding the additional penalty of one stroke** prescribed by the Rule and using as the reference point the point where the original ball last crossed the margin of the *hazard* before it came to rest in the *hazard*; or

(iii)   **add an additional penalty of one stroke** and play a ball as nearly as possible at the spot from which the last *stroke* from outside the *hazard* was made (see Rule 20-5).

Darren Clarke attempts to play his ball which lies in a lateral water hazard. Lateral water hazards should be defined by red stakes or lines.

110

Note 1: When proceeding under Rule 26-2b, the player is not required to drop a ball under Rule 27-1 or 28a. If he does drop a ball, he is not required to play it. He may alternatively proceed under Rule 26-2b(ii) or (iii).

Note 2: If a ball played from within a *water hazard* is declared unplayable outside the *hazard*, nothing in Rule 26-2b precludes the player from proceeding under Rule 28b or c.

PENALTY FOR BREACH OF RULE:
Match play – Loss of hole; Stroke play – Two strokes.

RULE 26 INCIDENT

Standing on Carnoustie's 18th tee, in the final round of the 1999 Open Championship, Jean Van de Velde needed only a double bogey to become the first Frenchman to win the championship since 1907.

Minutes later, with his navy blue trousers rolled to his knees, he was standing in the Barry Burn contemplating his fate and his options under Rule 26.

Having played a driver from the tee, the Frenchman's ball had finished well right but safely on a peninsula created by a bend in the burn. Instead of laying up with his second, Van de Velde attempted to play a 2-iron to the distant green. His shot was a bit wayward and it ricocheted off a grandstand railing, the wall of the water hazard and finally settled behind the second crossing of the burn in heavy rough.

Attempting to hit his ball out of the rough and over the burn, he played it badly and the ball finished in the shallow water of the burn. As the stream runs perpendicular to the line of play, it was marked with a yellow line indicating a water hazard.

As such, Van de Velde had three options. He could play the ball without penalty as it lay. Under penalty of one stroke, he could play again from where he last played, or he could drop behind the hazard keeping the point at which his ball last crossed the margin of the water hazard directly between the hole and the spot on which the ball would be dropped, with no limit to how far behind the hazard he might want to go.

Three in the water, and needing a six to win The Open, the Frenchman contemplated playing out of the hazard in order to avoid the penalty stroke. To make such an assessment, he decided to go into the water to see what the shot required. Having removed his shoes and socks, Van de Velde rolled up his trouser legs and lowered himself down the stone wall into the shallow water.

Van de Velde was left standing alone in the dark water, wedge in hand, assessing his ability to play the submerged ball out of the hazard. After several minutes, discretion became the better part of valour and Van de Velde chose option b under Rule 26-1. He dropped a ball behind the hazard on the stipulated line, suffered a penalty stroke and played his fifth shot to the right greenside bunker. His up-and-down from the bunker resulted in a score of seven and a play-off between himself, Paul Lawrie and Justin Leonard, which Lawrie went on to win.

RULE **27** | # BALL LOST OR OUT OF BOUNDS; PROVISIONAL BALL

DEFINITIONS

All defined terms are in *italics* and are listed alphabetically in the Definitions section – see pages 6–15.

See **incident** involving the Definition of "Lost Ball" on page 115–116

27-1. BALL LOST OR OUT OF BOUNDS

If a ball is *lost* or is *out of bounds*, the player must play a ball, **under penalty of one stroke**, as nearly as possible at the spot from which the original ball was last played (see Rule 20-5).

Exceptions:

1. If there is reasonable evidence that the original ball is *lost* in a *water hazard*, the player must proceed in accordance with Rule 26-1.

2. If there is reasonable evidence that the original ball is *lost* in an *obstruction* (Rule 24-3) or an *abnormal ground condition* (Rule 25-1c) the player may proceed under the applicable Rule.

PENALTY FOR BREACH OF RULE 27-1:
Match play – Loss of hole; Stroke play – Two strokes.

27-2. PROVISIONAL BALL
a. Procedure

If a ball may be *lost* outside a *water hazard* or may be *out of bounds*, to save time the player may play another ball provisionally in accordance with Rule 27-1. The player must inform his opponent in match play or his *marker* or a *fellow-competitor* in stroke play that he intends to play a *provisional ball*,

PLAYERS UNABLE TO IDENTIFY THEIR BALLS

My ball is a number 3 with black writing.

So is mine. Unless we can identify which is which, both balls are 'lost'.

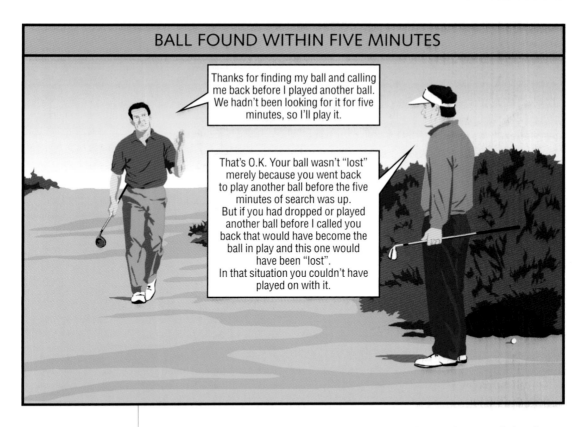

and he must play it before he or his *partner* goes forward to search for the original ball.

If he fails to do so and plays another ball, that ball is not a *provisional ball* and becomes the *ball in play* **under penalty of stroke and distance** (Rule 27-1); the original ball is *lost*.

(Order of play from teeing ground – see Rule 10-3)

Note: If a *provisional ball* played under Rule 27-2a might be *lost* outside a *water hazard* or *out of bounds*, the player may play another *provisional ball*. If another *provisional ball* is played, it bears the same relationship to the previous *provisional ball* as the first *provisional ball* bears to the original ball.

b. When Provisional Ball Becomes Ball in Play

The player may play a *provisional ball* until he reaches the place where the original ball is likely to be. If he makes a *stroke* with the *provisional ball* from the place where the original ball is likely to be or from a point nearer the *hole* than that place, the original ball is *lost* and the *provisional ball* becomes the *ball in play* **under penalty of stroke and distance** (Rule 27-1).

If the original ball is *lost* outside a *water hazard* or is *out of bounds*, the *provisional ball* becomes the *ball in play*, **under penalty of stroke and distance** (Rule 27-1).

If there is reasonable evidence that the original ball is *lost* in a *water hazard*, the player must proceed in accordance with Rule 26-1.

Exception: If there is reasonable evidence that the original ball is *lost* in an *obstruction* (Rule 24-3) or an *abnormal ground condition* (Rule 25-1c) the player may proceed under the applicable Rule.

113

PROVISIONAL BALL BECOMES BALL IN PLAY

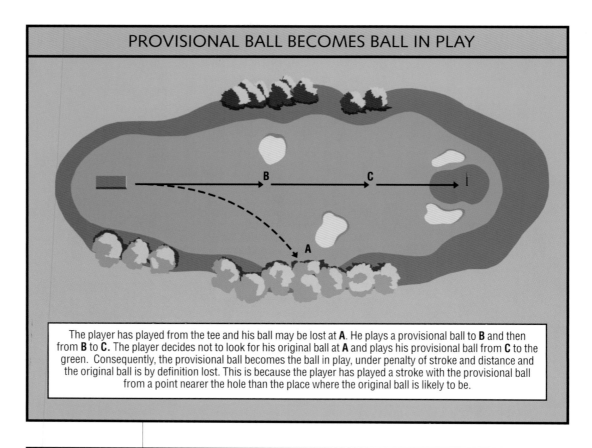

The player has played from the tee and his ball may be lost at **A**. He plays a provisional ball to **B** and then from **B** to **C.** The player decides not to look for his original ball at **A** and plays his provisional ball from **C** to the green. Consequently, the provisional ball becomes the ball in play, under penalty of stroke and distance and the original ball is by definition lost. This is because the player has played a stroke with the provisional ball from a point nearer the hole than the place where the original ball is likely to be.

PROVISIONAL BALL PLAYED: ORIGINAL BALL FOUND UNPLAYABLE

A player plays a provisional ball as his ball may be lost. The original ball is found within five minutes and before the provisional ball has become the ball in play, but the ball is unplayable. The player must abandon the provisional ball and proceed with the original ball.

c. When Provisional Ball to be Abandoned

If the original ball is neither *lost* nor *out of bounds*, the player must abandon the *provisional ball* and continue play with the original ball. If he makes any further *strokes* at the *provisional ball*, he is playing a *wrong ball* and the provisions of Rule 15 apply.

Note: If a player plays a *provisional ball* under Rule 27-2a, the *strokes* made after this Rule has been invoked with a *provisional ball* subsequently abandoned under Rule 27-2c and *penalty strokes* incurred solely by playing that ball are disregarded.

RULE 27 INCIDENT

During the third round of the 1998 Open Championship at Royal Birkdale, Mark O'Meara's second shot drifted too far to the right into knee high grass and gorse at the 480-yard 6th hole and put into motion a series of events that led to the introduction of a clarifying Decision.

By the time O'Meara and his caddie reached the area where they thought his ball had landed, a number of spectators were already engaged in searching for it. The Rules observer with the group started the clock for the five-minute search period when O'Meara and his caddie arrived.

Several balls were found, but none were O'Meara's. To everyone in the immediate vicinity, he announced the type of ball he was using and stated that it was embossed with his logo.

After searching for approximately four minutes, O'Meara suspected that his ball was lost. He left the search area, took another ball from his caddie, and started back down the fairway to play again from where his original ball had been played.

About 30 seconds later, a spectator announced, 'Here it is. I have it'. Someone called to O'Meara, who apparently did not hear and continued walking. An official went to where the spectator had found the ball and saw it was the type O'Meara was using and did have his logo on it.

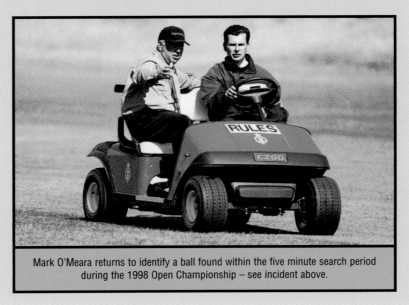

Mark O'Meara returns to identify a ball found within the five minute search period during the 1998 Open Championship – see incident above.

By this time, it was nearing the end of the five-minute search period permitted under the Rules, and it was clear that O'Meara would not be able to get back to the ball in order to identify it within the five-minute period. The Definition of "Lost Ball" states that a ball is lost if it is not "found or identified" within five minutes. If the definition said "found and identified", the procedure would have been clear. A radio call was made for a roving Rules official to make a decision.

The roving official arrived on the scene and brought O'Meara in a cart back up the fairway where a discussion took place. A further official arrived and it was determined that the ball had been found within the five-minute period, that O'Meara was entitled to identify it outside the stipulated time period and, if it was his ball, he was entitled to play it so everyone returned to the area where the ball had been found.

However, during the search, the search area had been trampled and a misguided spectator, who believed the ball had been abandoned, had lifted it. When O'Meara and the official went to the spot, the ball was not there but the spectator was close by and returned the ball to O'Meara who identified it as his. Although the spectator said he knew "exactly" where the ball had been before he lifted it that turned out to be only an approximation.

Under Rules 18-1 and 20-3c, O'Meara was required to drop as nearly as possible to the spot where the ball had been before being lifted by the spectator. When O'Meara dropped the ball, it rolled more than two club-lengths from the spot where it struck a part of the course thus requiring a re-drop. Upon re-dropping, the ball rolled nearer to the hole and O'Meara, therefore, placed it on the spot where it first struck a part of the course when re-dropped. He then played his shot and continued the round, winning the championship the following day.

The ambiguity of the Definition of "Lost Ball", in this particular situation, necessitated the addition of Decision 27/5.5. The new decision simply clarifies that if a ball is found within five minutes, the player is allowed enough time to reach the area and identify it even though the identification takes place after the five-minute search period has elapsed.

RULE 28 · BALL UNPLAYABLE

DEFINITIONS

See **incident** involving Rule 28 on page 118–119

All defined terms are in *italics* and are listed alphabetically in the Definitions section – see pages 6–15.

The player may deem his ball unplayable at any place on the *course* except when the ball is in a *water hazard*. The player is the sole judge as to whether his ball is unplayable.

If the player deems his ball to be unplayable, he must, **under penalty of one stroke**:

a. Play a ball as nearly as possible at the spot from which the original ball was last played (see Rule 20-5); or

BALL UNPLAYABLE IN BUNKER: PLAYER'S OPTIONS

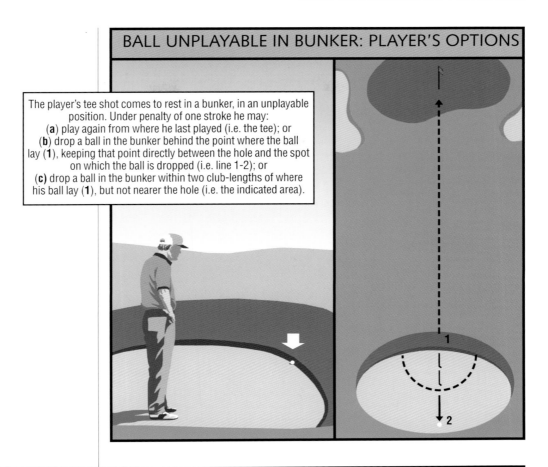

The player's tee shot comes to rest in a bunker, in an unplayable position. Under penalty of one stroke he may:
(**a**) play again from where he last played (i.e. the tee); or
(**b**) drop a ball in the bunker behind the point where the ball lay (**1**), keeping that point directly between the hole and the spot on which the ball is dropped (i.e. line 1-2); or
(**c**) drop a ball in the bunker within two club-lengths of where his ball lay (**1**), but not nearer the hole (i.e. the indicated area).

BALL UNPLAYABLE IN BUSH: PLACE FOR DROPPING

My ball was in the bush. I've declared it unplayable, and I'm going to invoke option **c** and drop the ball within two club-lengths of where it lay.

That's O.K. But remember the ball when dropped must strike a part of the course within two club-lengths of where it lay.

b. Drop a ball behind the point where the ball lay, keeping that point directly between the *hole* and the spot on which the ball is dropped, with no limit to how far behind that point the ball may be dropped; or

c. Drop a ball within two club-lengths of the spot where the ball lay, but not nearer the *hole*.

If the unplayable ball is in a *bunker*, the player may proceed under Clause a, b or c. If he elects to proceed under Clause b or c, a ball must be dropped in the *bunker*.

The ball may be lifted and cleaned when proceeding under this Rule.

PENALTY FOR BREACH OF RULE:
Match play – Loss of hole; Stroke play – Two strokes.

RULE 28 INCIDENT

A ball may be declared unplayable anywhere upon the course except in a water hazard. However, whether a ball lies in a bunker or not can have an important impact upon the player's options, as Corey Pavin discovered at the 1992 U.S. Open at Pebble Beach.

While it is a question of fact as to where a ball actually lies on the course, it sometimes takes close inspection to be certain. At the 11th hole, Pavin's ball found its way under the grassy lip of a fairway bunker. At such a position it was not readily evident whether it was in the bunker or through the green.

The definition of a bunker excludes the grass-covered ground bordering or within the hazard. The margin of the bunker extends vertically downwards but not upward, and a ball is in a bunker when

During the 1992 US Open Championship, Corey Pavin calls for assistance to determine whether his ball lies in a bunker at the 11th hole.

it lies in or any part of it touches the bunker.

By asking for a ruling, Pavin wanted to determine where he was permitted to drop his ball under the provisions of Rule 28 in addition to taking a stroke and distance penalty. If his ball were not in the bunker, he would be permitted to drop outside the bunker under penalty of one stroke. If his ball were in the bunker, his only dropping option would be within the bunker.

After close examination, it was ruled that the ball was in the bunker. Pavin declared it unplayable and dropped in the hazard, keeping the point where the ball lay directly between the hole and the spot on which the ball was dropped. He incurred a one penalty stroke penalty under Rule 28.

RULE 29   THREESOMES AND FOURSOMES

DEFINITIONS

All defined terms are in *italics* and are listed alphabetically in the Definitions section – see pages 6–15.

See **incident** involving Rule 29 on page 121–122

29-1. GENERAL

In a *threesome* or a *foursome*, during any *stipulated round* the *partners* must play alternately from the *teeing grounds* and alternately during the play of each hole. *Penalty strokes* do not affect the order of play.

29-2. MATCH PLAY

If a player plays when his *partner* should have played, **his *side* loses the hole**.

119

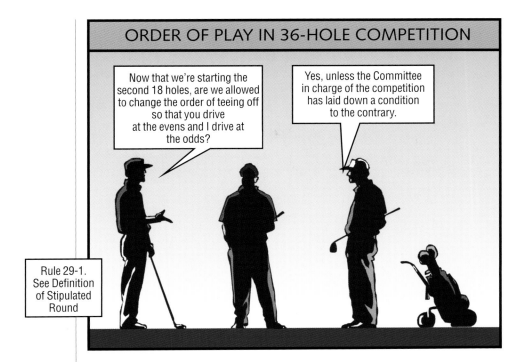

ORDER OF PLAY IN 36-HOLE COMPETITION

Now that we're starting the second 18 holes, are we allowed to change the order of teeing off so that you drive at the evens and I drive at the odds?

Yes, unless the Committee in charge of the competition has laid down a condition to the contrary.

Rule 29-1. See Definition of Stipulated Round

29-3. STROKE PLAY

If the *partners* make a *stroke* or *strokes* in incorrect order, such *stroke* or *strokes* are cancelled and **the *side* incurs a penalty of two strokes**. The *side* must correct the error by playing a ball in correct order as nearly as possible at the spot from which it first played in incorrect order (see Rule 20-5). If the *side* makes a *stroke* on the next *teeing ground* without first correcting the error or, in the case of the last hole of the round, leaves the *putting green* without declaring its intention to correct the error, **the *side* is disqualified**.

RULE 29 INCIDENT

The practice putting green at the Old Course in St Andrews lies just off the course and only a few steps from the 1st tee. Paired together on the second day for the morning foursomes of the 1975 Walker Cup Match, the U.S. side of veteran William C. Campbell and newcomer John Grace reported to the tee a little ahead of time. They had already decided that Grace would drive at the odd numbered holes, so Campbell decided to use the extra time before the match began to walk to the practice green and hit a few putts.

As the visiting team, Campbell and Grace had the honour. The wind was blowing from the west off St Andrews Bay, which carried the announcement of the match's beginning beyond Campbell's earshot.

As the breeze momentarily died, Campbell heard "the click" of Grace's drive just before striking a practice putt, and he was unable to interrupt his stroke. He had practised during the play of the hole. Instantly and instinctively recognising his breach, Campbell walked onto the fairway and reported to the Referee that the U.S. had lost the first hole. [Rule 7-2 and Rule 29.]

The referee for the match accepted Campbell's report but made no immediate announcement to the other players. Because play of the hole had ended with the breach of Rule 7-2, Campbell was free to play his side's second from where Grace's good drive lay to the green, as simply more practice.

Walking across the Swilken Burn, Campbell told Grace what had taken place. "He was incredulous, to say the least," Campbell recalls.

The Americans lost the first hole and eventually lost the match to Mark James and Richard Eyles.

RULE **30** THREE-BALL, BEST-BALL AND FOUR-BALL MATCH PLAY

DEFINITIONS All defined terms are in *italics* and are listed alphabetically in the Definitions section – see pages 6–15.

30-1. RULES OF GOLF APPLY
The Rules of Golf, so far as they are not at variance with the following specific Rules, apply to *three-ball*, *best-ball* and *four-ball matches*.

30-2. THREE-BALL MATCH PLAY
a. Ball at Rest Moved by an Opponent
Except as otherwise provided in the *Rules*, if the player's ball is touched or *moved* by an opponent, his *caddie* or *equipment* other than during search, Rule 18-3b applies. **That opponent incurs a penalty of one stroke in his match with the player**, but not in his match with the other opponent.

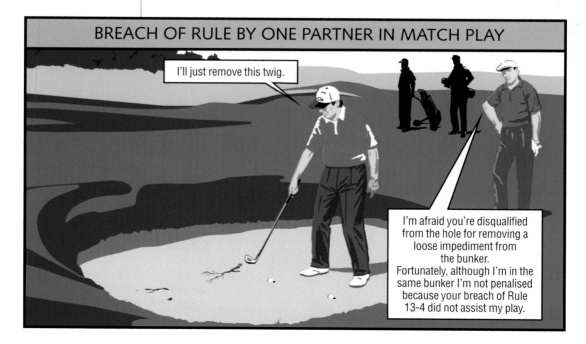

BREACH OF RULE BY ONE PARTNER IN MATCH PLAY

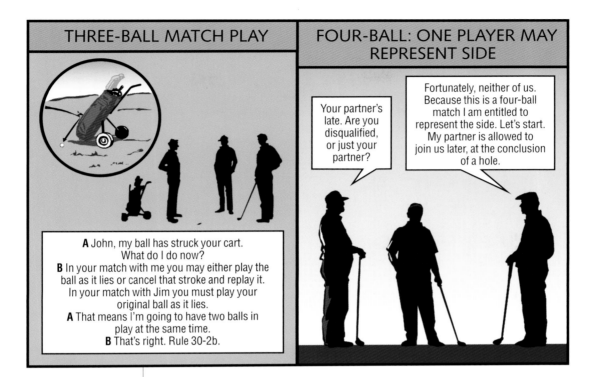

THREE-BALL MATCH PLAY

A John, my ball has struck your cart. What do I do now?
B In your match with me you may either play the ball as it lies or cancel that stroke and replay it. In your match with Jim you must play your original ball as it lies.
A That means I'm going to have two balls in play at the same time.
B That's right. Rule 30-2b.

FOUR-BALL: ONE PLAYER MAY REPRESENT SIDE

Your partner's late. Are you disqualified, or just your partner?

Fortunately, neither of us. Because this is a four-ball match I am entitled to represent the side. Let's start. My partner is allowed to join us later, at the conclusion of a hole.

b. Ball Deflected or Stopped by an Opponent Accidentally

If a player's ball is accidentally deflected or stopped by an opponent, his *caddie* or *equipment*, there is no penalty. In his match with that opponent the player may play the ball as it lies or, before another *stroke* is played by either *side*, he may cancel the *stroke* and play a ball without penalty as nearly as possible at the spot from which the original ball was last played (see Rule 20-5). In his match with the other opponent, the ball must be played as it lies.

Exception: Ball striking person attending *flagstick* – see Rule 17-3b.
(Ball purposely deflected or stopped by opponent – see Rule 1-2)

30-3. BEST-BALL AND FOUR-BALL MATCH PLAY
a. Representation of Side

A *side* may be represented by one *partner* for all or any part of a match; all *partners* need not be present. An absent *partner* may join a match between holes, but not during play of a hole.

b. Maximum of Fourteen Clubs

The *side* is penalised for a breach of Rules 4-3a(iii) and 4-4 by any *partner*.

c. Order of Play

Balls belonging to the same *side* may be played in the order the *side* considers best.

d. Wrong Ball

If a player makes a *stroke* at a *wrong ball* that is not in a *hazard*, **he is disqualified for that hole**, but his *partner* incurs no penalty even if the *wrong*

123

ball belongs to him. If the *wrong ball* belongs to another player, its owner must place a ball on the spot from which the *wrong ball* was first played.

e. Disqualification of Side
(i) **A *side* is disqualified** for a breach of any of the following by any *partner*:

Rule 1-3	Agreement to Waive Rules
Rule 4-1 or -2	Clubs
Rule 5-1 or -2	The Ball
Rule 6-2a	Handicap (playing off higher handicap)
Rule 6-4	Caddie (having more than one caddie; failure to correct breach immediately)
Rule 6-7	Undue Delay; Slow Play (repeated offence)
Rule 14-3	Artificial Devices and Unusual Equipment

(ii) **A *side* is disqualified** for a breach of any of the following by all *partners*:

Rule 6-3	Time of Starting and Groups
Rule 6-8	Discontinuance of Play

(iii) In all other cases where a breach of a *Rule* would result in disqualification, **the player is disqualified for that hole only.**

f. Effect of Other Penalties
If a player's breach of a *Rule* assists his *partner's* play or adversely affects an opponent's play, **the *partner* incurs the applicable penalty in addition to any penalty incurred by the player.**

In all other cases where a player incurs a penalty for breach of a *Rule*, the penalty does not apply to his *partner*. Where the penalty is stated to be loss of hole, the effect is to disqualify the player for that hole.

g. Another Form of Match Played Concurrently
In a *best-ball* or *four-ball* match when another form of match is played concurrently, the above specific Rules apply.

RULE 31 FOUR-BALL STROKE PLAY

DEFINITIONS

All defined terms are in *italics* and are listed alphabetically in the Definitions section – see pages 6–15.

31-1. GENERAL
In *four-ball* stroke play two *competitors* play as *partners*, each playing his own ball. The lower score of the *partners* is the score for the hole. If one *partner* fails to complete the play of a hole, there is no penalty.

The Rules of Golf, so far as they are not at variance with the following specific Rules, apply to *four-ball* stroke play.

31-2. REPRESENTATION OF SIDE
A *side* may be represented by either *partner* for all or any part of a *stipulated round*; both *partners* need not be present. An absent *competitor* may join his *partner* between holes, but not during play of a hole.

FOUR-BALL STROKE PLAY

Date __3RD APRIL 1996__

Competition __SPRING OPEN FOUR-BALL__

PLAYER A __J. SUTHERLAND__ Handicap __16__ Strokes __12__

PLAYER B __W. B. TAYLOR__ Handicap __12__ Strokes __9__

Hole	Length Yards	Par	Stroke Index	Gross Score A	Gross Score B	Net Score A	Net Score B	Won X Lost – Half O	Mar. Score	Hole	Length Yards	Par	Stroke Index	Gross Score A	Gross Score B	Net Score A	Net Score B	Won X Lost – Half O	Mar. Score
1	437	4	4			4	3			10	425	4	3	5		4			
2	320	4	14			4	4			11	141	3	17	3		3			
3	162	3	18			4	4			12	476	5	9	6		5			
4	504	5	7	6		5				13	211	3	11		4		4		
5	181	3	16	4		4				14	437	4	5		5		4		
6	443	4	2		5	4				15	460	4	1		5		4		
7	390	4	8		5	4				16	176	3	15	4		4			
8	346	4	12	5		4				17	340	4	13	4		4			
9	340	4	10	4		3				18	435	4	6	6		5			
Out	3123	35					35			In	3101	34					37		
										Out	3123	35					35		
										T'tl	6224	69					72		
										Handicap									
										Net Score									

Player's Signature __J. Sutherland__

Marker's Signature __R. J. Parker__

PARTNERS' SCORES TO BE INDIVIDUALLY IDENTIFIED

1. The lower score of the partners is the score for the hole(Rule 31)

2. Only one of the partners need be responsible for complying with Rule 6-6b i.e. recording scores, checking scores, countersigning and returning the card (Rule 31-4).

3. The competitor is solely responsible for the correctness of the gross score recorded. Although there is no objection to the competitor (or his marker) entering the net score, it is the Committee's responsibility to record the better ball score for each hole, to add up the scores and to apply the handicaps recorded on the card (Rule 33-5). Thus there is no penalty for an error by the competitor (or his marker) for recording an incorrect net score.

4. Scores of the two partners must be kept in separate columns otherwise it is impossible for the Committee to apply the correct handicap. If the scores of both partners, having different handicaps, are recorded in the same column, the Committee has no alternative but to disqualify both partners (Rules 31-7 and 6-6 apply).

5. The Committee is responsible for laying down the conditions under which a competition is to be played (Rule 33-1), including the method of handicapping. In the above illustration the Committee laid down that ¾ handicaps would apply.

31-3. MAXIMUM OF FOURTEEN CLUBS

The *side* is penalised for a breach of Rules 4-3a (iii) and 4-4 by either *partner*.

31-4. SCORING

The *marker* is required to record for each hole only the gross score of whichever *partner's* score is to count. The gross scores to count must be individually identifiable; otherwise **the *side* is disqualified**. Only one of the *partners* need be responsible for complying with Rule 6-6b.
(Wrong score – see Rule 31-7a)

31-5. ORDER OF PLAY

Balls belonging to the same *side* may be played in the order the *side* considers best.

31-6. WRONG BALL

If a *competitor* makes a *stroke* at a *wrong ball* that is not in a *hazard*, **he incurs a penalty of two strokes** and must correct his mistake by playing the correct ball or by proceeding under the *Rules*. His *partner* incurs no penalty even if the *wrong ball* belongs to him.

   If the *wrong ball* belongs to another *competitor*, its owner must place a ball on the spot from which the *wrong ball* was first played.

31-7. DISQUALIFICATION PENALTIES
a. Breach by One Partner
A *side* is disqualified from the competition for a breach of any of the following by either *partner*:

Rule 1-3	Agreement to Waive Rules
Rule 3-4	Refusal to Comply with Rule
Rule 4-1 or -2	Clubs
Rule 5-1 or -2	The Ball
Rule 6-2b	Handicap (playing off higher handicap; failure to record handicap)
Rule 6-4	Caddie (having more than one caddie; failure to correct breach immediately)
Rule 6-6b	Signing and Returning Score Card
Rule 6-6d	Wrong Score for Hole, i.e. when the recorded score of the *partner* whose score is to count is lower than actually taken. If the recorded score of the *partner* whose score is to count is higher than actually taken, it must stand as returned
Rule 6-7	Undue Delay; Slow Play (repeated offence)
Rule 7-1	Practice Before or Between Rounds
Rule 14-3	Artificial Devices and Unusual Equipment
Rule 31-4	Gross Scores to Count Not Individually Identifiable

b. Breach by Both Partners
A *side* is disqualified:
(i)   for a breach by both of Rule 6-3 (Time of Starting and Groups) or Rule 6-8 (Discontinuance of Play), or

(ii)   if, at the same hole, each *partner* is in breach of a *Rule* the penalty for which is disqualification from the competition or for a hole.

c. For the Hole Only

In all other cases where a breach of a *Rule* would result in disqualification, **the competitor is disqualified only for the hole at which the breach occurred**.

31-8. EFFECT OF OTHER PENALTIES

If a *competitor's* breach of a *Rule* assists his *partner's* play, **the partner incurs the applicable penalty in addition to any penalty incurred by the competitor**.

In all other cases where a *competitor* incurs a penalty for breach of a *Rule*, the penalty does not apply to his *partner*.

RULE

DEFINITIONS

BOGEY, PAR AND STABLEFORD COMPETITIONS

All defined terms are in *italics* and are listed alphabetically in the Definitions section – see pages 6–15.

32-1. CONDITIONS

Bogey, par and Stableford competitions are forms of stroke play in which play is against a fixed score at each hole. The *Rules* for stroke play, so far as they are not at variance with the following specific Rules, apply.

a. Bogey and Par Competitions

The scoring for bogey and par competitions is made as in match play. Any hole for which a *competitor* makes no return is regarded as a loss. The winner is the *competitor* who is most successful in the aggregate of holes.

The *marker* is responsible for marking only the gross number of *strokes* for each hole where the *competitor* makes a net score equal to or less than the fixed score.

Note 1: Maximum of Fourteen Clubs – Penalties as in match play – see Rule 4-4
Note 2: One Caddie at Any One Time – Penalties as in match play – see Rule 6-4
Note 3: Undue Delay; Slow Play (Rule 6-7) – The *competitor's* score is adjusted by deducting one hole from the overall result.

b. Stableford Competitions

The scoring in Stableford competitions is made by points awarded in relation to a fixed score at each hole as follows:

Hole Played In	Points
More than one over fixed score or no score returned	0
One over fixed score	1
Fixed score	2
One under fixed score	3
Two under fixed score	4
Three under fixed score	5
Four under fixed score	6

The winner is the *competitor* who scores the highest number of points.

The *marker* is responsible for marking only the gross number of *strokes* at each hole where the *competitor's* net score earns one or more points.

Note 1: Maximum of Fourteen Clubs (Rule 4-4) – Penalties applied as follows: From total points scored for the round, deduction of two points for each hole at which any breach occurred; maximum deduction per round: four points.

Note 2: One Caddie at Any One Time (Rule 6-4) – Penalties applied as follows: From the points scored for the round; deduction of two points for each hole at which any breach occurred; maximum deduction per round: four points.

Note 3: Undue Delay; Slow Play (Rule 6-7) – The *competitor's* score is adjusted by deducting two points from the total points scored for the round.

32-2. DISQUALIFICATION PENALTIES
a. From the Competition
A *competitor* **is disqualified** from the competition for a breach of any of the following:

Rule 1-3	Agreement to Waive Rules
Rule 3-4	Refusal to Comply with Rule
Rule 4-1 or -2	Clubs
Rule 5-1 or -2	The Ball
Rule 6-2b	Handicap (playing off higher handicap; failure to record handicap)
Rule 6-3	Time of Starting and Groups
Rule 6-4	Caddie (having more than one caddie; failure to correct breach immediately)
Rule 6-6b	Signing and Returning Score Card
Rule 6-6d	Wrong Score for Hole, i.e. when the recorded score is lower than actually taken, except that no penalty is incurred when a breach of this Rule does not affect the result of the hole
Rule 6-7	Undue Delay; Slow Play (repeated offence)
Rule 6-8	Discontinuance of Play
Rule 7-1	Practice Before or Between Rounds
Rule 14-3	Artificial Devices and Unusual Equipment

b. For a Hole
In all other cases where a breach of a *Rule* would result in disqualification, **the *competitor* is disqualified only for the hole at which the breach occurred.**

RULE  33

THE COMMITTEE

DEFINITIONS

All defined terms are in *italics* and are listed alphabetically in the Definitions section – see pages 6–15.

See **incident** involving Rule 33-1 on page 131–132

33-1. CONDITIONS; WAIVING RULE
The *Committee* must establish the conditions under which a competition is to be played.

The *Committee* has no power to waive a Rule of Golf.

Certain specific *Rules* governing stroke play are so substantially different from those governing match play that combining the two forms of play is not practicable and is not permitted. The results of *matches* played and the scores returned in these circumstances must not be accepted.

In stroke play the *Committee* may limit a *referee's* duties.

33-2. THE COURSE
a. Defining Bounds and Margins
The *Committee* must define accurately:

(i) the *course* and *out of bounds*,

(ii) the margins of *water hazards* and *lateral water hazards*,

(iii) *ground under repair*, and

(iv) *obstructions* and integral parts of the *course*.

b. New Holes
New *holes* should be made on the day on which a stroke play competition begins and at such other times as the *Committee* considers necessary, provided all *competitors* in a single round play with each *hole* cut in the same position.

Exception: When it is impossible for a damaged *hole* to be repaired so that it conforms with the Definition, the *Committee* may make a new *hole* in a nearby similar position.

Note: Where a single round is to be played on more than one day, the *Committee* may provide in the conditions of a competition that the *holes* and *teeing grounds* may be differently situated on each day of the competition, provided that, on any one day, all *competitors* play with each *hole* and each *teeing ground* in the same position.

If the course is not in a playable condition, the Committee may have to temporarily suspend play. In stroke play only, if further play becomes impossible, the Committee may have to declare play null and void.

c. Practice Ground

Where there is no practice ground available outside the area of a competition *course*, the *Committee* should establish the area on which players may practise on any day of a competition, if it is practicable to do so. On any day of a stroke play competition, the *Committee* should not normally permit practice on or to a *putting green* or from a *hazard* of the competition *course*.

d. Course Unplayable

If the *Committee* or its authorised representative considers that for any reason the *course* is not in a playable condition or that there are circumstances that render the proper playing of the game impossible, it may, in match play or stroke play, order a temporary suspension of play or, in stroke play, declare play null and void and cancel all scores for the round in question. When a round is cancelled, all penalties incurred in that round are cancelled. (Procedure in discontinuing and resuming play – see Rule 6-8)

33-3. TIMES OF STARTING AND GROUPS

The *Committee* must establish the times of starting and, in stroke play, arrange the groups in which *competitors* must play.

When a match play competition is played over an extended period, the *Committee* establishes the limit of time within which each round must be completed. When players are allowed to arrange the date of their match within these limits, the *Committee* should announce that the match must be played at a stated time on the last day of the period unless the players agree to a prior date.

33-4. HANDICAP STROKE TABLE

The *Committee* must publish a table indicating the order of holes at which handicap *strokes* are to be given or received.

33-5. SCORE CARD

In stroke play, the *Committee* must provide each *competitor* with a score card containing the date and the *competitor's* name or, in *foursome* or *four-ball* stroke play, the *competitors'* names.

In stroke play, the *Committee* is responsible for the addition of scores and application of the handicap recorded on the score card.

In *four-ball* stroke play, the *Committee* is responsible for recording the better-ball score for each hole and in the process applying the handicaps recorded on the score card, and adding the better-ball scores.

In bogey, par and Stableford competitions, the *Committee* is responsible for applying the handicap recorded on the score card and determining the result of each hole and the overall result or points total.

Note: The *Committee* may request that each *competitor* records the date and his name on his score card.

33-6. DECISION OF TIES

The *Committee* must announce the manner, day and time for the decision of a halved match or of a tie, whether played on level terms or under handicap.

A halved match must not be decided by stroke play. A tie in stroke play must not be decided by a match.

33-7. DISQUALIFICATION PENALTY; COMMITTEE DISCRETION

A penalty of disqualification may in exceptional individual cases be waived, modified or imposed if the *Committee* considers such action warranted.

Any penalty less than disqualification must not be waived or modified.

If a *Committee* considers that a player is guilty of a serious breach of etiquette, it may impose a penalty of disqualification under this Rule.

33-8. LOCAL RULES

a. Policy

See **incident** involving Rule 33-8 below

The *Committee* may establish Local Rules for local abnormal conditions if they are consistent with the policy set forth in Appendix I.

b. Waiving or Modifying a Rule

A Rule of Golf must not be waived by a Local Rule. However, if a *Committee* considers that local abnormal conditions interfere with the proper playing of the game to the extent that it is necessary to make a Local Rule that modifies the Rules of Golf, the Local Rule must be authorised by the *R&A*.

RULE 33 INCIDENTS

Nick Faldo learned the hard way that it is always a good idea to ascertain which Local Rules have been adopted for a competition and, just as importantly, which have not.

The Royal and Ancient Golf Club of St. Andrews and the PGA European Tour have for years employed in their championships a Local Rule allowing the removal of stones in bunkers by declaring the stones to be movable obstructions. Faldo was accustomed to playing under such a Local Rule.

In the autumn of 1994, however, he ran into trouble in a bunker during the third round of the Alfred Dunhill Masters in Bali. Believing erroneously that the removal of stones was sanctioned in the Bali event as it was on the European tour, Faldo employed the Local Rule during the third round.

On the following day, a competitor was almost penalised for removing a stone in a bunker. The player's confusion stemmed from the fact that Faldo had removed a stone from a bunker the previous day.

Leading the tournament by six strokes with just six holes remaining, Faldo was called off the course. The three-time Open Champion and two-time Masters Champion had, of course, returned his score card for the third round and as it did not include the two penalty strokes for his breach of Rule 13-4, he was disqualified.

In the 3rd round of the 2000 Weetabix Women's British Open Championship at Royal Birkdale Golf Club, Karrie Webb took incorrect relief from a fixed sprinkler head on her line of play.

Webb was entitled to relief from the fixed sprinkler head within two club-lengths of the putting green by a Local Rule and together with her fellow-competitor, Trish Johnson, Webb referred to the wording of the Local Rule contained in Appendix I of the Rules of Golf. Having read the Local Rule Webb confirmed that she was entitled to relief. She determined her nearest point of relief but then mistakenly measured a one club-length area within which to drop the ball. Webb was required to drop at the nearest point of relief and having dropped and played the ball from within one club-length of this point rather than at it, Webb was in breach of the Local Rule and incurred a penalty of two strokes.

Rules officials in the Championship office noticed the infringement on the television coverage but could not prevent the breach occurring. Webb was advised of the infringement and resulting penalty at the conclusion of her round but before she signed her score card, thereby avoiding a disqualification for signing for a score lower than actually taken.

RULE 34 | DISPUTES AND DECISIONS

DEFINITIONS

All defined terms are in *italics* and are listed alphabetically in the Definitions section – see pages 6–15.

34-1. CLAIMS AND PENALTIES
a. Match Play
If a claim is lodged with the *Committee* under Rule 2-5, a decision should be given as soon as possible so that the state of the match may, if necessary, be adjusted. If a claim is not made in accordance with Rule 2-5, it must not be considered by the *Committee*.

There is no time limit on applying the disqualification penalty for a breach of Rule 1-3.

See **incident** involving Rule 34-1b on page 133

b. Stroke Play
In stroke play, a penalty must not be rescinded, modified or imposed after the competition has closed. A competition is closed when the result has been officially announced or, in stroke play qualifying followed by match play, when the player has teed off in his first match.

Exceptions: A penalty of disqualification must be imposed after the competition has closed if a *competitor*:

(i)   was in breach of Rule 1-3 (Agreement to Waive Rules); or
(ii)   returned a score card on which he had recorded a handicap that, before the competition closed, he knew was higher than that to which he was entitled, and this affected the number of strokes received (Rule 6-2b); or
(iii) returned a score for any hole lower than actually taken (Rule 6-6d) for any reason other than failure to include a penalty that, before the competition closed, he did not know he had incurred; or
(iv)   knew, before the competition closed, that he had been in breach of any other *Rule* for which the penalty is disqualification.

34-2. REFEREE'S DECISION

If a *referee* has been appointed by the *Committee*, his decision is final.

34-3. COMMITTEE'S DECISION

In the absence of a *referee*, any dispute or doubtful point on the *Rules* must be referred to the *Committee*, whose decision is final.

If the *Committee* cannot come to a decision, it may refer the dispute or doubtful point to the Rules of Golf Committee of the *R&A*, whose decision is final.

If the dispute or doubtful point has not been referred to the Rules of Golf Committee, the player or players may request that an agreed statement be referred through a duly authorised representative of the *Committee* to the Rules of Golf Committee for an opinion as to the correctness of the decision given. The reply will be sent to this authorised representative.

If play is conducted other than in accordance with the Rules of Golf, the Rules of Golf Committee will not give a decision on any question.

RULE 34 INCIDENT

A case involving Mark O'Meara at the 1997 Lancôme Trophy provided a good example of the operation of Rule 34-1b. Video evidence came to light a considerable time after the competition had closed which demonstrated that during the final round O'Meara, having marked and lifted his ball on the putting green, mistakenly and unknown to himself, replaced his ball in a wrong place marginally closer to the hole.

If O'Meara's error had been noticed prior to the player returning his card, O'Meara would have been penalised two strokes at the hole concerned for playing from a wrong place (Rule 20-7b). If the breach had come to light after O'Meara had returned his card, but prior to the competition closing, the Committee would have had no choice but to disqualify him under Rule 6-6d as his score for the hole was lower than actually taken due to failure to include the penalty.

However, Rule 34-1b provides that except in the four situations listed under the Rule, the Committee may not impose, rescind or modify a penalty after the competition has closed and, as O'Meara's mistake came to light after the result of the competition had been announced this meant that no penalty was imposed by the Committee. The results stood as played, with O'Meara the winner of the Tournament by one stroke.

APPENDIX I

CONTENTS

LOCAL RULES AND CONDITIONS OF THE COMPETITION

PART A LOCAL RULES

As provided in Rule 33-8a, the *Committee* may make and publish Local Rules for local abnormal conditions if they are consistent with the policy established in this Appendix. In addition, detailed information regarding acceptable and prohibited Local Rules is provided in "Decisions on the Rules of Golf" under Rule 33-8 and in "Guidance on Running a Competition".

If local abnormal conditions interfere with the proper playing of the game and the *Committee* considers it necessary to modify a Rule of Golf, authorisation from the *R&A* must be obtained.

1. DEFINING BOUNDS AND MARGINS

Specifying means used to define *out of bounds, water hazards, lateral water hazards, ground under repair, obstructions* and integral parts of the *course* (Rule 33-2a).

2. WATER HAZARDS
a. Lateral Water Hazards.

Clarifying the status of *water hazards* that may be *lateral water hazards* (Rule 26).

b. Provisional Ball.

Permitting play of a *provisional ball* under Rule 26-1 for a ball that may be in a *water hazard* of such character that if the original ball is not found, there is reasonable evidence that it is *lost* in the *water hazard* and it would be impracticable to determine whether the ball is in the *hazard* or to do so would unduly delay play. The ball is played provisionally under any of the available options under Rule 26-1 or any applicable Local Rule. In such a case, if a *provisional ball* is played and the original ball is in a *water hazard*, the player may play the original ball as it lies or continue with the *provisional ball* in play, but he may not proceed under Rule 26-1 with regard to the original ball.

3. AREAS OF THE COURSE REQUIRING PRESERVATION; ENVIRONMENTALLY-SENSITIVE AREAS

Assisting preservation of the *course* by defining areas, including turf nurseries, young plantations and other parts of the *course* under cultivation as *"ground under repair"* from which play is prohibited.

When the *Committee* is required to prohibit play from environmentally-sensitive areas that are on or adjoin the *course*, it should make a Local Rule clarifying the relief procedure.

4. TEMPORARY CONDITIONS – MUD, EXTREME WETNESS, POOR CONDITIONS AND PROTECTION OF COURSE
a. Lifting an Embedded Ball, Cleaning

Temporary conditions that might interfere with proper playing of the game, including mud and extreme wetness, warranting relief for an embedded ball anywhere *through the green* or permitting lifting, cleaning and replacing a ball anywhere *through the green* or on a closely-mown area *through the green*.

b. "Preferred Lies" and "Winter Rules"

Adverse conditions, including the poor condition of the *course* or the existence of mud, are sometimes so general, particularly during winter months, that the *Committee* may decide to grant relief by temporary Local Rule either to protect the *course* or to promote fair and pleasant play. The Local Rule must be withdrawn as soon as the conditions warrant.

5. OBSTRUCTIONS
a. General

Clarifying status of objects that may be *obstructions* (Rule 24).

Declaring any construction to be an integral part of the *course* and, accordingly, not an

135

obstruction, e.g., built-up sides of *teeing grounds*, *putting greens* and *bunkers* (Rules 24 and 33-2a).

b. Stones in Bunkers
Allowing the removal of stones in *bunkers* by declaring them to be "movable *obstructions*" (Rule 24-1).

c. Roads and Paths
(i)   Declaring artificial surfaces and sides of roads and paths to be integral parts of the *course*, or
(ii) Providing relief of the type afforded under Rule 24-2b from roads and paths not having artificial surfaces and sides if they could unfairly affect play.

d. Immovable Obstructions Close to Putting Green
Providing relief from intervention by immovable *obstructions* on or within two club-lengths of the *putting green* when the ball lies within two club-lengths of the *obstruction*.

e. Protection of Young Trees
Providing relief for the protection of young trees.

f. Temporary Obstructions
Providing relief from interference by temporary *obstructions* (e.g., grandstands, television cables and equipment, etc).

6. DROPPING ZONES (BALL DROPS)
Establishing special areas on which balls may or must be dropped when it is not feasible or practicable to proceed exactly in conformity with Rule 24-2b or 24-3 (Immovable Obstruction), Rule 25-1b or 25-1c (Abnormal Ground Conditions), Rule 25-3 (Wrong Putting Green), Rule 26-1 (Water Hazards and Lateral Water Hazards) or Rule 28 (Ball Unplayable).

PART B SPECIMEN LOCAL RULES
Within the policy established in Part A of this Appendix, the *Committee* may adopt a Specimen Local Rule by referring, on a score card or notice board, to the examples given below. However, Specimen Local Rules 3a, 3b, 3c, 6a and 6b should not be printed or

referred to on a score card as they are all of limited duration.

1. AREAS OF THE COURSE REQUIRING PRESERVATION; ENVIRONMENTALLY-SENSITIVE AREAS
a. Ground Under Repair; Play Prohibited
If the *Committee* wishes to protect any area of the *course*, it should declare it to be *ground under repair* and prohibit play from within that area. **The following Local Rule is recommended:** "The _____(defined by ____) is *ground under repair* from which play is prohibited. If a player's ball lies in the area, or if it interferes with the player's *stance* or the area of his intended swing, the player must take relief under Rule 25-1.

PENALTY FOR BREACH OF LOCAL RULE:
**Match play – Loss of hole;
Stroke play – Two strokes."**

b. Environmentally-Sensitive Areas
If an appropriate authority (i.e. a Government Agency or the like) prohibits entry into and/or play from an area on or adjoining the *course* for environmental reasons, the *Committee* should make a Local Rule clarifying the relief procedure.

The *Committee* has some discretion in terms of whether the area is defined as *ground under repair*, a *water hazard* or *out of bounds*. However, it may not simply define the area to be a *water hazard* if it does not meet the Definition of a *"Water Hazard"* and it should attempt to preserve the character of the hole. **The following Local Rule is recommended:**

"**I. Definition**
An environmentally-sensitive area is an area so declared by an appropriate authority, entry into and/or play from which is prohibited for environmental reasons. These areas may be defined as *ground under repair*, a *water hazard*, a *lateral water hazard* or *out of bounds* at the discretion of the *Committee* provided that, in the case of an environmentally-sensitive area which has been defined as a *water hazard* or a *lateral water hazard*, the area is, by Definition, a *water hazard*. **Note:** The *Committee* may not declare an area to be environmentally-sensitive.

The Links course at Spanish Bay in California has areas of sand dunes which have been declared environmentally-sensitive. A player may not play from or enter these areas.

II. Ball in Environmentally-Sensitive Area
a. Ground Under Repair

If a ball is in an environmentally-sensitive area that is defined as *ground under repair*, a ball must be dropped in accordance with Rule 25-1b.

If there is reasonable evidence that a ball is *lost* within an environmentally-sensitive area that is defined as *ground under repair*, the player may take relief without penalty as prescribed in Rule 25-1c.

b. Water Hazards and Lateral Water Hazards

If a ball is in or there is reasonable evidence that it is *lost* in an environmentally-sensitive area that is defined as a *water hazard* or *lateral water hazard*, the player must, under penalty of one stroke, proceed under Rule 26-1.

Note: If a ball, dropped in accordance with Rule 26 rolls into a position where the environmentally-sensitive area interferes with the player's *stance* or the area of his intended swing, the player must take relief as provided in Clause III of this Local Rule.

c. Out of Bounds

If a ball is in an environmentally-sensitive area that is defined as *out of bounds*, the player must play a ball, under penalty of one stroke, as nearly as possible at the spot from which the original ball was last played (see Rule 20-5).

III. Interference with Stance or Area of Intended Swing

Interference by an environmentally-sensitive area occurs when the condition interferes with the player's *stance* or the area of his intended swing. If interference exists, the player must take relief as follows:

(a) **Through the Green:** If the ball lies *through the green*, the point on the *course* nearest to where the ball lies must be determined that (a) is not nearer the *hole*, (b) avoids interference by the condition and (c) is not in a *hazard* or on a *putting green*. The player must lift the ball and drop it without penalty within one club-length of the point so determined on a part of the *course* that fulfills (a), (b) and (c) above.

(b) **In a Hazard:** If the ball is in a *hazard*, the player must lift the ball and drop it either:

(i) Without penalty, in the *hazard*, as near as possible to the spot where the ball lay, but not nearer the *hole*, on a part of the *course* that provides complete relief from the condition; or

(ii) Under penalty of one stroke, outside the *hazard*, keeping the point where the ball lay directly between the *hole* and the spot on which the ball is dropped, with no limit to how far behind the *hazard* the ball may be dropped. Additionally, the player may proceed under Rule 26 or 28 if applicable.

(c) **On the Putting Green:** If the ball lies on the *putting green*, the player must lift the ball and

137

place it without penalty in the nearest position to where it lay that affords complete relief from the condition, but not nearer the *hole* or in a *hazard*. The ball may be cleaned when lifted under Clause III of this Local Rule.

Exception: A player may not obtain relief under Clause III of this Local Rule if (a) it is clearly unreasonable for him to make a *stroke* because of interference by anything other than a condition covered by this Local Rule or (b) interference by the condition would occur only through use of an unnecessarily abnormal *stance*, swing or direction of play.

PENALTY FOR BREACH OF LOCAL RULE:
**Match play – Loss of hole;
Stroke play – Two strokes.**

Note: In the case of a serious breach of this Local Rule, the *Committee* may impose a penalty of disqualification."

2. PROTECTION OF YOUNG TREES

When it is desired to prevent damage to young trees, **the following Local Rule is recommended**:

"Protection of young trees identified by _____ – If such a tree interferes with a player's *stance* or the area of his intended swing, the ball must be lifted, without penalty, and dropped in accordance with the procedure prescribed in Rule 24-2b (Immovable *Obstruction*). If the ball lies in a *water hazard*, the player must lift and drop the ball in accordance with Rule 24-2b(i) except that the *nearest point of relief* must be in the *water hazard* and the ball must be dropped in the *water hazard* or the player may proceed under Rule 26. The ball may be cleaned when lifted under this Local Rule.

Exception: A player may not obtain relief under this Local Rule if (a) it is clearly unreasonable for him to make a *stroke* because of interference by anything other than the tree or (b) interference by the tree would occur only through use of an unnecessarily abnormal *stance*, swing or direction of play.

PENALTY FOR BREACH OF LOCAL RULE:
**Match play – Loss of hole;
Stroke play – Two strokes.**"

3. TEMPORARY CONDITIONS – MUD, EXTREME WETNESS, POOR CONDITIONS AND PROTECTION OF THE COURSE

a. Relief for Embedded Ball; Cleaning Ball

Rule 25-2 provides relief without penalty for a ball embedded in its own pitch-mark in any closely-mown area *through the green*. On the *putting green*, a ball may be lifted and damage caused by the impact of a ball may be repaired (Rules 16-1b and c). When permission to take relief for an embedded ball anywhere *through the green* would be warranted, **the following Local Rule is recommended**:

"*Through the green*, a ball that is embedded in its own pitch-mark in the ground, other than sand, may be lifted without penalty, cleaned and dropped as near as possible to where it lay but not nearer the *hole*. The ball when dropped must first strike a part of the *course through the green*.

Exception: A player may not obtain relief under this Local Rule if it is clearly unreasonable for him to make a *stroke* because of interference by anything other than the condition covered by this Local Rule.

PENALTY FOR BREACH OF LOCAL RULE:
**Match play – Loss of hole;
Stroke play – Two strokes.**"

Alternatively, conditions may be such that permission to lift, clean and replace the ball will suffice. In these circumstances, **the following Local Rule is recommended**:

"(Specify area) a ball may be lifted, cleaned and replaced without penalty.

Note: The position of the ball must be marked before it is lifted under this Local Rule – see Rule 20-1.

PENALTY FOR BREACH OF LOCAL RULE:
**Match play – Loss of hole;
Stroke play – Two strokes.**"

b. "Preferred Lies" and "Winter Rules"

Ground under repair is provided for in Rule 25 and occasional local abnormal conditions that might interfere with fair play and are not widespread should be defined as *ground under repair*.

However, adverse conditions, such as heavy snows, spring thaws, prolonged rains or

RELIEF FROM STAKED TREES

The staked tree interferes with my swing. I must take relief according to the Local Rules, but my nearest point of relief leaves me blocked by the big tree.

I am afraid that is just bad luck. You must drop your ball within one club-length of the nearest point of relief.

extreme heat can make fairways unsatisfactory and sometimes prevent use of heavy mowing equipment. When such conditions are so general throughout a *course* that the *Committee* believes "preferred lies" or "winter rules" would promote fair play or help protect the course, **the following Local Rule is recommended**:

"A ball lying on a closely-mown area *through the green* [or specify a more restricted area, e.g. at the 6th hole] may be lifted without penalty and cleaned. Before lifting the ball, the player must mark its position. Having lifted the ball, he must place it on a spot within [specify area, e.g. six inches, one club-length, etc.] of and not nearer the *hole* than where it originally lay, that is not in a *hazard* and not on a *putting green*.

A player may place his ball only once, and it is in play when it has been placed (Rule 20-4). If the ball fails to come to rest on the spot on which it is placed, Rule 20-3d applies. If the ball when placed comes to rest on the spot on which it is placed and it subsequently *moves*, there is no penalty and the ball must be played as it lies, unless the provisions of any other *Rule* apply.

If the player fails to mark the position of the ball before lifting it or *moves* the ball in any

other manner, such as rolling it with a club, he incurs a penalty of one stroke.

*PENALTY FOR BREACH OF LOCAL RULE
Match play – Loss of hole;
Stroke play – Two strokes

*If a player incurs the general penalty for a breach of this Local Rule, no additional penalty under the Local Rule is applied."

c. Aeration Holes

When a *course* has been aerated, a Local Rule permitting relief, without penalty, from an aeration hole may be warranted. **The following Local Rule is recommended**:

"*Through the green*, a ball that comes to rest in or on an aeration hole may be lifted without penalty, cleaned and dropped, as near as possible to the spot where it lay but not nearer the *hole*. The ball when dropped must first strike a part of the *course through the green*.

On the *putting green*, a ball that comes to rest in or on an aeration hole may be placed at the nearest spot not nearer the *hole* that avoids the situation.

PENALTY FOR BREACH OF LOCAL RULE:
Match play – Loss of hole;
Stroke play – Two strokes."

139

4. STONES IN BUNKERS

Stones are, by definition, *loose impediments* and, when a player's ball is in a *hazard*, a stone lying in or touching the *hazard* may not be touched or moved (Rule 13-4). However, stones in *bunkers* may represent a danger to players (a player could be injured by a stone struck by the player's club in an attempt to play the ball) and they may interfere with the proper playing of the game.

When permission to lift a stone in a *bunker* would be warranted, **the following Local Rule is recommended**:

"Stones in *bunkers* are movable *obstructions* (Rule 24-1 applies)."

5. IMMOVABLE OBSTRUCTIONS CLOSE TO PUTTING GREEN

Rule 24-2 provides relief without penalty from interference by an immovable *obstruction*, but it also provides that, except on the *putting green*, intervention on the *line of play* is not, of itself, interference under this Rule.

However, on some courses, the aprons of the *putting greens* are so closely mown that players may wish to putt from just off the green. In such conditions, immovable obstructions on the apron may interfere with the proper playing of the game and the introduction of **the following Local Rule providing additional relief without penalty from intervention by an** immovable *obstruction* **would be warranted**:

"Relief from interference by an immovable *obstruction* may be obtained under Rule 24-2. In addition, if a ball lies off the *putting green* but not in a *hazard* and an immovable *obstruction* on or within two club-lengths of the *putting green* and within two club-lengths of the ball intervenes on the *line of play* between the ball and the *hole*, the player may take relief as follows:

The ball must be lifted and dropped at the nearest point to where the ball lay that (a) is not nearer the *hole*, (b) avoids intervention and (c) is not in a *hazard* or on a *putting green*. The ball may be cleaned when lifted.

Relief under this Local Rule is also available if the player's ball lies on the *putting green* and an immovable *obstruction* within two club-lengths of the *putting green* intervenes on his *line of putt*. The player may take relief as follows: The ball must be lifted and placed at the nearest point where the ball lay that (a) is not nearer the *hole*, (b) avoids intervention and (c) is not in a *hazard*. The ball may be cleaned when lifted.

PENALTY FOR BREACH OF LOCAL RULE:
Match play – Loss of hole;
Stroke play – Two strokes."

6. TEMPORARY OBSTRUCTIONS

When temporary *obstructions* are installed on or adjoining the *course*, the *Committee* should

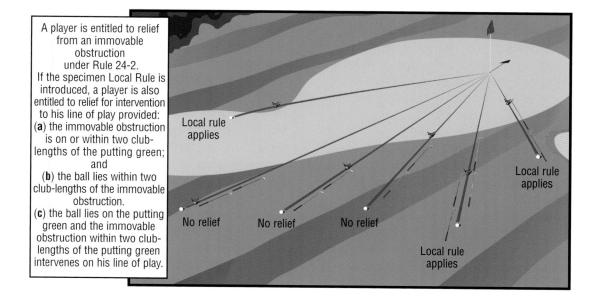

A player is entitled to relief from an immovable obstruction under Rule 24-2.
If the specimen Local Rule is introduced, a player is also entitled to relief for intervention to his line of play provided:
(**a**) the immovable obstruction is on or within two club-lengths of the putting green; and
(**b**) the ball lies within two club-lengths of the immovable obstruction.
(**c**) the ball lies on the putting green and the immovable obstruction within two club-lengths of the putting green intervenes on his line of play.

define the status of such *obstructions* as movable, immovable or temporary immovable *obstructions*.

a. Temporary Immovable Obstructions
If the *Committee* defines such *obstructions* as temporary immovable *obstructions*, **the following Local Rule is recommended**:

"I. Definition
A temporary immovable *obstruction* is a non-permanent artificial object that is often erected in conjunction with a competition and is fixed or not readily movable.

Examples of temporary immovable *obstructions* include, but are not limited to, tents, scoreboards, grandstands, television towers and lavatories.

Supporting guy wires are part of the temporary immovable *obstruction* unless the *Committee* declares that they are to be treated as elevated power lines or cables.

II. Interference
Interference by a temporary immovable *obstruction* occurs when (a) the ball lies in front of and so close to the *obstruction* that the *obstruction* interferes with the player's *stance* or the area of his intended swing, or (b) the ball lies in, on, under or behind the *obstruction* so that any part of the *obstruction* intervenes directly between the player's ball and the *hole*; interference also exists if the ball lies within one club-length of a spot equidistant from the hole where such intervention would exist.

Note: A ball is under a temporary immovable *obstruction* when it is below the outer most edges of the *obstruction*, even if these edges do not extend downwards to the ground.

III. Relief
A player may obtain relief from interference by a temporary immovable *obstruction*, including a temporary immovable *obstruction* that is *out of bounds*, as follows:
(a) **Through the Green:** If the ball lies *through the green*, the point on the *course* nearest to where the ball lies must be determined that (a) is not nearer the *hole*, (b) avoids interference as defined in Clause II and (c) is not in a *hazard* or

on a *putting green*. The player must lift the ball and drop it without penalty within one club-length of the point so determined on a part of the *course* that fulfills (a), (b) and (c) above.
(b) **In a Hazard:** If the ball is in a *hazard*, the player must lift and drop the ball either:
(i) Without penalty, in accordance with Clause IIIa above, except that the nearest part of the *course* affording complete relief must be in the *hazard* and the ball must be dropped in the *hazard* or, if complete relief is impossible, on a part of the *course* within the *hazard* that affords maximum available relief; or
(ii) Under penalty of one stroke, outside the *hazard* as follows: the point on the *course* nearest to where the ball lies must be determined that (a) is not nearer the *hole*, (b) avoids interference as defined in Clause II and (c) is not in a *hazard*. The player must drop the ball within one club-length of the point so determined on a part of the *course* that fulfills (a), (b) and (c) above.

The ball may be cleaned when lifted under Clause III.
Note 1: If the ball lies in a *hazard*, nothing in this Local Rule precludes the player from proceeding under Rule 26 or Rule 28, if applicable.
Note 2: If a ball to be dropped under this Local Rule is not immediately recoverable, another ball may be *substituted*.
Note 3: A *Committee* may make a Local Rule (a) permitting or requiring a player to use a dropping zone or ball drop when taking relief from a temporary immovable *obstruction* or (b) permitting a player, as an additional relief option, to drop the ball on the opposite side of the *obstruction* from the point established under Clause III, but otherwise in accordance with Clause III.
Exceptions: If a player's ball lies in front of or behind the temporary immovable *obstruction* (not in, on or under the *obstruction*) he may not obtain relief under Clause III if:
1. It is clearly unreasonable for him to make a *stroke* or, in the case of intervention, to make a *stroke* such that the ball could finish on a direct line to the *hole*, because of interference by anything other than the

If there are temporary immovable obstructions, such as TV towers, on the course, the Committee should introduce a Local Rule providing for relief from such temporary immovable obstructions.

temporary immovable *obstruction*;
2. Interference by the temporary immovable *obstruction* would occur only through use of an unnecessarily abnormal *stance*, swing or direction of play; or
3. In the case of intervention, it would be clearly unreasonable to expect the player to be able to strike the ball far enough towards the *hole* to reach the temporary immovable *obstruction*.

Note: A player not entitled to relief due to these exceptions may proceed under Rule 24-2, if applicable.

IV. Ball Lost

If there is reasonable evidence that the ball is *lost* in, on or under a temporary immovable *obstruction*, a ball may be dropped under the provisions of Clause III or Clause V, if applicable.

For the purpose of applying Clauses III and V, the ball is deemed to lie at the spot where it last crossed the outermost limits of the *obstruction* (Rule 24-3).

V. Dropping Zones (Ball Drops)

If the player has interference from a temporary immovable *obstruction*, the *Committee* may permit or require the use of a dropping zone or ball drop. If the player uses a dropping zone in taking relief, he must drop the ball in the dropping zone nearest to where his ball originally lay or is deemed to lie under Clause IV (even though the nearest dropping zone may be nearer the *hole*).

Note 1: A *Committee* may make a Local Rule prohibiting the use of a dropping zone or ball drop that is nearer the *hole*.

Note 2: If the ball is dropped in a dropping zone, the ball must not be re-dropped if it comes to rest within two club-lengths of the spot where it first struck a part of the *course* even though it may come to rest nearer the *hole* or outside the boundaries of the dropping zone.

**PENALTY FOR BREACH OF LOCAL RULE:
Match play – Loss of hole;
Stroke play – Two strokes."**

b. Temporary Power Lines and Cables

When temporary power lines, cables, or telephone lines are installed on the *course*, **the following Local Rule is recommended:**

"Temporary power lines, cables, telephone lines and mats covering or stanchions supporting them are *obstructions*:
1. If they are readily movable, Rule 24-1 applies.
2. If they are fixed or not readily movable, the player may, if the ball lies *through the green* or in a *bunker*, obtain relief as provided in Rule 24-2b. If the ball lies in a *water hazard*, the player may lift and drop the ball in accordance with Rule 24-2b(i) except that the *nearest point of relief* must be in the *water hazard* and the ball must be dropped in the *water hazard* or the player may proceed under Rule 26.
3. If a ball strikes an elevated power line or cable, the *stroke* must be cancelled and replayed, without penalty (see Rule 20-5). If the ball is not immediately recoverable another ball may be *substituted*.

Note: Guy wires supporting a temporary immovable *obstruction* are part of the temporary immovable *obstruction* unless the *Committee*, by Local Rule, declares that they are to be treated as elevated power lines or cables.

Exception: Ball striking elevated junction section of cable rising from the ground must not be replayed.

4. Grass-covered cable trenches are *ground under repair* even if not marked and Rule 25-1b applies."

PART C CONDITIONS OF THE COMPETITION

Rule 33-1 provides, "The *Committee* must establish the conditions under which a competition is to be played." The conditions should include many matters such as method of entry, eligibility, number of rounds to be played, etc. which it is not appropriate to deal with in the Rules of Golf or this Appendix. Detailed information regarding these conditions is provided in "Decisions on the Rules of Golf" under Rule 33-1 and in "Guidance on Running a Competition".

However, there are a number of matters that might be covered in the Conditions of the Competition to which the *Committee's* attention is specifically drawn.
These are:

1. SPECIFICATION OF THE BALL (NOTE TO RULE 5-1)

The following two conditions are recommended only for competitions involving expert players:

a. List of Conforming Golf Balls

The *R&A* periodically issues a List of Conforming Golf Balls which lists balls that have been tested and found to conform. If the *Committee* wishes to require players to play a brand of golf ball on the List, the List should be posted and **the following condition of competition used:**

"The ball the player plays must be named on the current List of Conforming Golf Balls issued by the *R&A*.

PENALTY FOR BREACH OF CONDITION: Disqualification."

b. One Ball Condition

If it is desired to prohibit changing brands and types of golf balls during a *stipulated round*, **the following condition is recommended:**

"Limitation on Balls Used During Round: (Note to Rule 5-1)

(i) "One Ball" Condition

During a *stipulated round*, the balls a player plays must be of the same brand and type as detailed by a single entry on the current List of Conforming Golf Balls.

Note: If a ball of a different brand and/or type is dropped or placed it may be lifted, without

penalty, and the player must then proceed by dropping or placing a proper ball (Rule 20-6).

PENALTY FOR BREACH OF CONDITION: Match Play – At the conclusion of the hole at which the breach is discovered, the state of the match must be adjusted by deducting one hole for each hole at which a breach occurred; maximum deduction per round: Two holes. Stroke Play – Two strokes for each hole at which any breach occurred; maximum penalty per round: Four strokes.

(ii) Procedure When Breach Discovered

When a player discovers that he has played a ball in breach of this condition, he must abandon that ball before playing from the next *teeing ground* and complete the round with a proper ball; otherwise, the player is disqualified. If discovery is made during play of a hole and the player elects to *substitute* a proper ball before completing that hole, the player must place a proper ball on the spot where the ball played in breach of the condition lay."

2. TIME OF STARTING (NOTE TO RULE 6-3a)

If the *Committee* wishes to act in accordance with the Note, **the following wording is recommended:**

"If the player arrives at his starting point, ready to play, within five minutes after his starting time, in the absence of circumstances that warrant waiving the penalty of disqualification as provided in Rule 33-7, the penalty for failure to start on time is loss of the first hole to be played in match play or two strokes in stroke play. Penalty for lateness beyond five minutes is disqualification."

3. CADDIE (NOTE TO RULE 6-4)

Rule 6-4 permits a player to use a *caddie* provided he has only one *caddie* at any one time. However, there may be circumstances where a *Committee* may wish to ban *caddies* or restrict a player in his choice of *caddie*, e.g. professional golfer, sibling, parent, another player in the competition, etc. In such cases,

143

the following wording is recommended:

Use of Caddie Prohibited

"A player is prohibited from using a *caddie* during the *stipulated round*."

Restriction on Who May Serve as Caddie

"A player is prohibited from having _____ serve as his *caddie* during the *stipulated round*.

PENALTY FOR BREACH OF CONDITION:

Match play – At the conclusion of the hole at which the breach is discovered, the state of the match is adjusted by deducting one hole for each hole at which a breach occurred; maximum deduction per round – Two holes.

Stroke play – Two strokes for each hole at which any breach occurred; maximum penalty per round – Four strokes.

Match or stroke play – In the event of a breach between the play of two holes, the penalty applies to the next hole.

A player having a *caddie* in breach of this condition must immediately upon discovery that a breach has occurred ensure that he conforms with this condition for the remainder of the *stipulated round*. Otherwise, the player is disqualified."

4. PACE OF PLAY (NOTE 2 TO RULE 6-7)

The *Committee* may establish pace of play guidelines to help prevent slow play, in accordance with Note 2 to Rule 6-7.

5. SUSPENSION OF PLAY DUE TO A DANGEROUS SITUATION (NOTE TO RULE 6-8b)

As there have been many deaths and injuries from lightning on golf courses, all clubs and sponsors of golf competitions are urged to take precautions for the protection of persons against lightning. Attention is called to Rules 6-8 and 33-2d. If the *Committee* desires to adopt the condition in the Note under Rule 6-8b, **the following wording is recommended:**

"When play is suspended by the *Committee* for a dangerous situation, if the players in a match or group are between the play of two holes, they must not resume play until the *Committee* has ordered a resumption of play. If they are in the process of playing a hole, they must discontinue play immediately and not resume play until the *Committee* has ordered a resumption of play. If a player fails

SUSPENSION OF PLAY DUE TO A DANGEROUS SITUATION

to discontinue play immediately, he is disqualified unless circumstances warrant waiving the penalty as provided in Rule 33-7.

The signal for suspending play due to a dangerous situation will be a prolonged note of the siren."

The following signals are generally used and it is recommended that all *Committees* do similarly:
Discontinue Play Immediately: One prolonged note of siren
Discontinue Play: Three consecutive notes of siren, repeated
Resume Play: Two short notes of siren, repeated

6. PRACTICE

a. General

The *Committee* may make regulations governing practice in accordance with the Note to Rule 7-1, Exception (c) to Rule 7-2, Note 2 to Rule 7 and Rule 33-2c.

b. Practice Between Holes (Note 2 to Rule 7)

It is recommended that a condition of competition prohibiting practice putting or chipping on or near the *putting green* of the hole last played be introduced only in stroke play competitions.

The following wording is recommended:

"A player must not play any practice *stroke* on or near the *putting green* of the hole last played. If a practice *stroke* is played on or near the *putting green* of the hole last played, the player incurs a penalty of two strokes at the next hole, except that in the case of the last hole of the round, he incurs the penalty at that hole."

7. ADVICE IN TEAM COMPETITIONS (NOTE TO RULE 8)

If the *Committee* wishes to act in accordance with the Note under Rule 8, **the following wording is recommended:**

"In accordance with the Note to Rule 8 of the Rules of Golf, each team may appoint one person (in addition to the persons from whom *advice* may be asked under that Rule) who may give *advice* to members of that team. Such person (if it is desired to insert any restriction on who may be nominated insert such restriction here) must be identified to the *Committee* before giving *advice*."

8. NEW HOLES (NOTE TO RULE 33-2b)

The *Committee* may provide, in accordance with the Note to Rule 33-2b, that the *holes* and *teeing grounds* for a single round competition, being held on more than one day, may be differently situated on each day.

9. TRANSPORTATION

If it is desired to require players to walk in a competition, **the following condition is recommended:**

"Players must walk at all times during a *stipulated round*.

PENALTY FOR BREACH OF CONDITION:
Match play – At the conclusion of the hole at which the breach is discovered, the state of the match must be adjusted by deducting one hole for each hole at which a breach occurred. Maximum deduction per round: Two holes. Stroke play – Two strokes for each hole at which any breach occurred; maximum penalty per round: Four strokes. In the event of a breach between the play of two holes, the penalty applies to the next hole. Match or stroke play – Use of any unauthorised form of transportation must be discontinued immediately upon discovery that a breach has occurred. Otherwise, the player is disqualified."

10. ANTI-DOPING

The *Committee* may require, in the Conditions of Competition, that players comply with an anti-doping policy.

11. HOW TO DECIDE TIES

Rule 33-6 empowers the *Committee* to determine how and when a halved match or a stroke play tie is decided. The decision should be published in advance.

The *R&A* recommends:

Match Play

A match which ends all square should be played off hole by hole until one *side* wins a hole. The play-off should start on the hole where the match began. In a handicap match, handicap strokes should be allowed as in the prescribed round.

Stroke Play

(a) In the event of a tie in a scratch stroke play competition, a play-off is recommended. Such a play-off may be over 18 holes or a smaller number of holes as specified by the *Committee*. If that is not feasible or there is still a tie, a hole-by-hole play-off is recommended.

(b) In the event of a tie in a handicap stroke play competition, a play-off with handicaps is recommended. Such a play-off may be over 18 holes or a smaller number of holes as specified by the *Committee*. If the play-off is less than 18 holes the percentage of 18 holes to be played should be applied to the players' handicaps to determine their play-off handicaps. Handicap stroke fractions of one-half stroke or more should count as a full stroke and any lesser fraction should be disregarded.

(c) In either a scratch or handicap stroke play competition, if a play-off of any type is not feasible, matching score cards is recommended. The method of matching cards should be announced in advance. An acceptable method of matching cards is to determine the winner on the basis of the best score for the last nine holes. If the tying players have the same score for the last nine, determine the winner on the basis of the last six holes, last three holes and finally the 18th hole. If this method is used in a handicap stroke play competition, one-half, one-third, one-sixth, etc. of the handicaps should be deducted. Fractions should not be disregarded. If this method is used in a competition with a multiple tee start, it is recommended that the "last nine holes, last six holes, etc." is considered to be holes 10-18, 13-18, etc.

(d) If the conditions of the competition provide that ties are to be decided over the last nine, last six, last three and last hole, they should also provide what will happen if this procedure does not produce a winner.

12. DRAW FOR MATCH PLAY

Although the draw for match play may be completely blind or certain players may be distributed through different quarters or eighths, the General Numerical Draw is recommended if matches are determined by a qualifying round.

General Numerical Draw

For purposes of determining places in the draw, ties in qualifying rounds other than those for the last qualifying place are decided by the order in which scores are returned, with the first score to be returned receiving the lowest available number, etc. If it is impossible to determine the order in which scores are returned, ties are determined by a blind draw.

UPPER HALF	LOWER HALF	UPPER HALF	LOWER HALF
64 QUALIFIERS		**32 QUALIFIERS**	
1 vs. 64	2 vs. 63	1 vs. 32	2 vs. 31
32 vs. 33	31 vs. 34	16 vs. 17	15 vs. 18
16 vs. 49	15 vs. 50	8 vs. 25	7 vs. 26
17 vs. 48	18 vs. 47	9 vs. 24	10 vs. 23
8 vs. 57	7 vs. 58	4 vs. 29	3 vs. 30
25 vs. 40	26 vs. 39	13 vs. 20	14 vs. 19
9 vs. 56	10 vs. 55	5 vs. 28	6 vs. 27
24 vs. 41	23 vs. 42	12 vs. 21	11 vs. 22
4 vs. 61	3 vs. 62	**16 QUALIFIERS**	
29 vs. 36	30 vs. 35	1 vs. 16	2 vs.15
13 vs. 52	14 vs. 51	8 vs. 9	7 vs.10
20 vs. 45	19 vs. 46	4 vs. 13	3 vs.14
5 vs. 60	6 vs. 59	5 vs. 12	6 vs. 11
28 vs. 37	27 vs. 38	**8 QUALIFIERS**	
12 vs. 53	11 vs. 54	1 vs. 8	2 vs. 7
21 vs. 44	22 vs. 43	4 vs. 5	3 vs. 6

APPENDICES II & III

Any design in a club or ball which is not covered by Rules 4 and 5 and Appendices II and III, or which might significantly change the nature of the game, will be ruled on by the *R&A*.

The dimensions contained in Appendices II and III are referenced in imperial measurements.

A metric conversion is also referenced for information, calculated using a conversion rate of 1 inch = 25.4 mm. In the event of any dispute over the conformity of a club or ball, the imperial measurement takes precedence.

APPENDIX II

DESIGN OF CLUBS

A player in doubt as to the conformity of a club should consult the *R&A*.

A manufacturer should submit to the *R&A* a sample of a club, which is to be manufactured for a ruling as to whether the club conforms with the *Rules*. If a manufacturer fails to submit a sample or to await a ruling before manufacturing and/or marketing the club, the manufacturer assumes the risk of a ruling that the club does not conform with the *Rules*. Any sample submitted to the *R&A* becomes its property for reference purposes.

The following paragraphs prescribe general regulations for the design of clubs, together with specifications and interpretations. Further information relating to these regulations and their proper interpretation is provided in "A Guide to the Rules on Clubs and Balls".

Where a club, or part of a club, is required to have some specific property, this means that it must be designed and manufactured with the intention of having that property. The finished club or part must have that property within manufacturing tolerances appropriate to the material used.

1. CLUBS
a. General
A club is an implement designed to be used for striking the ball and generally comes in three forms: woods, irons and putters distinguished by shape and intended use. A putter is a club with a loft not exceeding ten degrees designed primarily for use on the *putting green*.

The club must not be substantially different from the traditional and customary form and make. The club must be composed of a shaft and a head. All parts of the club must be fixed so that the club is one unit, and it must have no external attachments except as otherwise permitted by the *Rules*.

b. Adjustability
Woods and irons must not be designed to be adjustable except for weight. Putters may be designed to be adjustable for weight and some other forms of adjustability are also permitted. All methods of adjustment permitted by the *Rules* require that:
(i)   the adjustment cannot be readily made;
(ii)   all adjustable parts are firmly fixed and there is no reasonable likelihood of them working loose during a round; and
(iii) all configurations of adjustment conform with the *Rules*.
The disqualification penalty for purposely changing the playing characteristics of a club during a *stipulated round* (Rule 4-2a) applies to all clubs including a putter.

c. Length
The overall length of the club must be at least 18 inches (457.2 mm) and, except for putters, must not exceed 48 inches (1,219.2 mm). For woods and irons, the measurement of length is taken when the club is lying on a horizontal plane and the sole is set against a 60 degree plane as shown in Fig. I. The length is defined as the

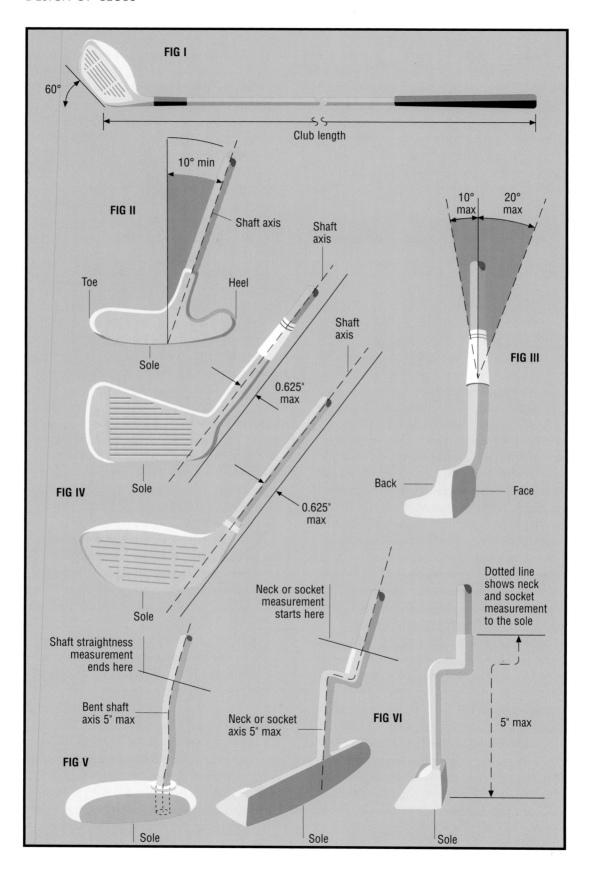

FIG I

60°

Club length

FIG II

10° min

Shaft axis

Toe

Heel

Sole

Shaft axis

Shaft axis

0.625" max

FIG III

10° max

20° max

Back

Face

FIG IV

Sole

Sole

0.625" max

Sole

Shaft straightness measurement ends here

Bent shaft axis 5" max

Neck or socket measurement starts here

Neck or socket axis 5" max

FIG VI

Dotted line shows neck and socket measurement to the sole

5" max

FIG V

Sole

Sole

Sole

distance from the point of the intersection between the two planes to the top of the grip. For putters, the measurement of length is taken from the top of the grip along the axis of the shaft or a straight line extension of it to the sole of the club. **Note:** Clubs in breach of the maximum length limit as specified in Appendix II, 1c, which were in use or marketed prior to 1st January 2004 and which otherwise conform to the *Rules*, may be used until 31st December 2004.

d. Alignment

When the club is in its normal address position the shaft must be so aligned that:

(i)   the projection of the straight part of the shaft on to the vertical plane through the toe and heel must diverge from the vertical by at least 10 degrees (see Fig. II);

(ii)   the projection of the straight part of the shaft on to the vertical plane along the intended line of play must not diverge from the vertical by more than 20 degrees forwards or 10 degrees backwards (see Fig. III).

Except for putters, all of the heel portion of the club must lie within 0.625 inches (15.88 mm) of the plane containing the axis of the straight part of the shaft and the intended (horizontal) line of play (see Fig. IV).

2. SHAFT

a. Straightness

The shaft must be straight from the top of the grip to a point not more than 5 inches (127 mm) above the sole, measured from the point where the shaft ceases to be straight along the axis of the bent part of the shaft and the neck and/or socket (see Fig. V).

b. Bending and Twisting Properties

At any point along its length, the shaft must:

(i)   bend in such a way that the deflection is the same regardless of how the shaft is rotated about its longitudinal axis; and

(ii)   twist the same amount in both directions.

c. Attachment to Clubhead

The shaft must be attached to the clubhead at the heel either directly or through a single plain neck and/or socket. The length from the top of the neck and/or socket to the sole of the club must not exceed 5 inches (127 mm), measured along the axis of, and following any bend in, the neck and/or socket (see Fig. VI).

Exception for Putters: The shaft or neck or socket of a putter may be fixed at any point in the head.

3. GRIP (see Fig. VII)

The grip consists of material added to the shaft to enable the player to obtain a firm hold. The grip must be straight and plain in form, must extend to the end of the shaft and must not be moulded for any part of the hands. If no material is added, that portion of the shaft designed to be held by the player must be considered the grip.

(i)   For clubs other than putters the grip must be circular in cross-section, except that a continuous, straight, slightly raised rib may be incorporated along the full length of the grip, and a slightly indented spiral is permitted on a wrapped grip or a replica of one.

(ii)   A putter grip may have a non-circular cross-section, provided the cross-section has no concavity, is symmetrical and remains generally similar throughout the length of the grip. (See Clause (v) below).

(iii)   The grip may be tapered but must not have any bulge or waist. Its cross-sectional dimensions measured in any direction must not exceed 1.75 inches (44.45 mm).

(iv)   For clubs other than putters the axis of the grip must coincide with the axis of the shaft.

(v)   A putter may have two grips provided each is circular in cross-section, the axis of each coincides with the axis of the shaft, and they are separated by at least 1.5 inches (38.1mm).

4. CLUBHEAD

a. Plain in Shape

The clubhead must be generally plain in shape. All parts must be rigid, structural in nature and functional. It is not practicable to define plain in shape precisely and comprehensively but features which are deemed to be in breach of this requirement and are therefore not permitted include:

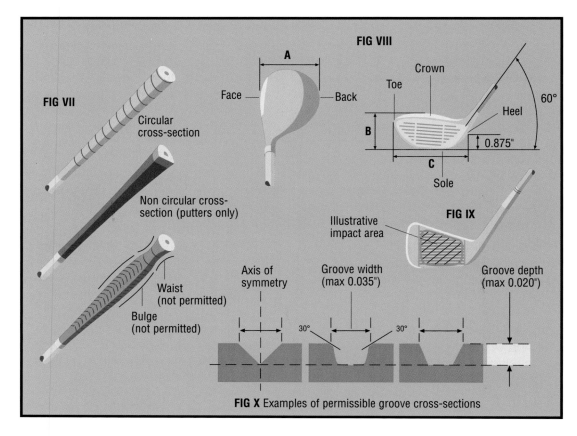

FIG VII

Circular cross-section

Non circular cross-section (putters only)

Waist (not permitted)

Bulge (not permitted)

FIG VIII

A

Face — — Back

Crown

Toe

Heel

60°

B

0.875"

C

Sole

Illustrative impact area

FIG IX

Axis of symmetry

Groove width (max 0.035")

Groove depth (max 0.020")

30° 30°

FIG X Examples of permissible groove cross-sections

(i)   holes through the head,

(ii)   transparent material added for other than decorative or structural purposes,

(iii) appendages to the main body of the head such as knobs, plates, rods or fins,

for the purpose of meeting dimensional specifications, for aiming or for any other purpose. Exceptions may be made for putters.

Any furrows in or runners on the sole must not extend into the face.

b. Dimensions and Size
(i) Woods

When the club is in a 60 degree lie angle, the dimensions of the clubhead must be such that:

(a)   the distance from the heel to the toe of the clubhead is greater than the distance from the face to the back;

(b)   the distance from the heel to the toe of the clubhead is not greater than 5 inches (127 mm); and

(c)   the distance from the sole to the crown of the clubhead is not greater than 2.8 inches (71.12 mm).

These dimensions are measured on horizontal lines between vertical projections of the outermost points of:

- the heel and the toe; and
- the face and the back (see Fig. VIII, dimension A);

and on vertical lines between the horizontal projections of the outermost points of the sole and the crown (see Fig. VIII, dimension B). If the outermost point of the heel is not clearly defined, it is deemed to be 0.875 inches (22.23 mm) above the horizontal plane on which the club is lying (see Fig. VIII, dimension C).

The size of the clubhead must not exceed 28.06 cubic inches (460 cubic centimetres), plus a tolerance of 0.61 cubic inches (10 cubic centimetres).

Note: Clubs in breach of the maximum size limit as specified in Appendix II, 4b (i), which were in use or marketed prior to 1st January 2004 and which otherwise conform to the *Rules*, may be used until 31st December 2004.

(ii) Irons and Putters

When the clubhead is in its normal address

position the dimensions of the head must be such that the distance from the heel to the toe is greater than the distance from the face to the back. For traditionally shaped heads, these dimensions will be measured on horizontal lines between vertical projections of the outermost points of:

- the heel and the toe; and
- the face and the back.

For unusually shaped heads, the toe to heel dimension may be made at the face.

c. Striking Faces

The clubhead must have only one striking face, except that a putter may have two such faces if their characteristics are the same, and they are opposite each other.

5. CLUB FACE

a. General

The material and construction of, or any treatment to, the face or clubhead must not have the effect at impact of a spring (test on file), or impart significantly more or less spin to the ball than a standard steel face, or have any other effect which would unduly influence the movement of the ball.

The face of the club must be hard and rigid (some exceptions may be made for putters) and, except for such markings listed below, must be smooth and must not have any degree of concavity.

b. Impact Area Roughness and Material

Except for markings specified in the following paragraphs, the surface roughness within the area where impact is intended (the "impact area") must not exceed that of decorative sandblasting, or of fine milling (see Fig. IX).

The whole of the impact area must be of the same material. Exceptions may be made for wooden clubs.

c. Impact Area Markings

Markings in the impact area must not have sharp edges or raised lips as determined by a finger test. Grooves or punch marks in the impact area must meet the following specifications:

(i) **Grooves.** A series of straight grooves with diverging sides and a symmetrical cross-section may be used (see Fig. X).

- The width and cross-section must be consistent across the face of the club and along the length of the grooves.
- Any rounding of groove edges must be in the form of a radius which does not exceed 0.020 inches (0.508 mm).
- The width of the grooves must not exceed 0.035 inches (0.9 mm), using the 30 degree method of measurement on file with the *R&A*.
- The distance between edges of adjacent grooves must not be less than three times the width of a groove, and not less than 0.075 inches (1.905 mm).
- The depth of a groove must not exceed 0.020 inches (0.508 mm).

(ii) **Punch Marks.** Punch marks may be used. The area of any such mark must not exceed 0.0044 square inches (2.84 sq. mm). A mark must not be closer to an adjacent mark than 0.168 inches (4.27 mm) measured from centre to centre. The depth of a punch mark must not exceed 0.040 inches (1.02 mm). If punch marks are used in combination with grooves, a punch mark must not be closer to a groove than 0.168 inches (4.27 mm), measured from centre to centre.

d. Decorative Markings

The centre of the impact area may be indicated by a design within the boundary of a square whose sides are 0.375 inches (9.53 mm) in length. Such a design must not unduly influence the movement of the ball. Decorative markings are permitted outside the impact area.

e. Non-metallic Club Face Markings

The above specifications apply to clubs on which the impact area of the face is of metal or a material of similar hardness. They do not apply to clubs with faces made of other materials and whose loft angle is 24 degrees or less, but markings which could unduly influence the movement of the ball are prohibited. Clubs with this type of face and a loft angle exceeding 24 degrees may have grooves of maximum width 0.040 inches (1.02 mm) and maximum depth 1½ times the groove width, but must otherwise conform to the markings specifications above.

f. Putter Face Markings
The specifications above with regard to roughness, material and markings in the impact area do not apply to putters.

APPENDIX III

THE BALL

1. WEIGHT
The weight of the ball shall not be greater than 1.620 ounces avoirdupois (45.93 gm).

2. SIZE
The diameter of the ball shall be not less than 1.680 inches (42.67 mm). This specification will be satisfied if, under its own weight, a ball falls through a 1.680 inches diameter ring gauge in fewer than 25 out of 100 randomly selected positions, the test being carried out at a temperature of 23 ± 1°C.

3. SPHERICAL SYMMETRY
The ball must not be designed, manufactured or intentionally modified to have properties which differ from those of a spherically symmetrical ball.

4. INITIAL VELOCITY
The initial velocity of the ball must not exceed the limit specified (test on file) when measured on apparatus approved by the R&A.

5. OVERALL DISTANCE STANDARD
The combined carry and roll of the ball, when tested on apparatus approved by the R&A, must not exceed the distance specified under the conditions set forth in the Overall Distance Standard for golf balls on file with the R&A.

HANDICAPS
The Rules of Golf do not legislate for the allocation and adjustment of handicaps. Such matters are within the jurisdiction of the National Union concerned and queries should be directed accordingly.

First published in 2003
by Hamlyn, a division of Octopus Publishing Group Ltd
2–4 Heron Quays, London E14 4JP

Text copyright © 2003 R&A Rules Limited
Design copyright © 2003 Octopus Publishing Group Ltd

All rights reserved. No part of this publication may be reproduced, stored in a retrieval system, or transmitted in any form or by any means, electronic, mechanical, photocopying, recording or otherwise, without the prior permission of the copyright holders.

ISBN 0 600 60890 5

A CIP catalogue record for this book is available from the British Library

Printed in Italy

10 9 8 7 6 5 4 3 2 1

PHOTOGRAPHIC ACKNOWLEDGEMENTS

Allsport 98 top left, / David Cannon 12, 30, 42, 76, 87 top, 115, 119, / Graham Chadwick 109 bottom, / Phil Cole 129, / Stephen Dunn 47, 55, / David Frost 92, / Craig Jones 87 bottom, / Warren Little 44, / Stephen Munday 7 bottom, 105, / Andrew Redington 30 bottom, 31, 35

Peter Dazeley 23 left, 98 top right

Joann Dost Golf Editions / Joann Dost 68 bottom

Hulton Getty Picture Collection 19

Phil Sheldon Golf Picture Library 7 top, 23 right, 50 top, 59, 97, 106, 136, 141

United States Golf Association 27 bottom

RULES INCIDENTS ACKNOWLEDGEMENT
Gary Galyean